Christianity, LGBTQ Suicide, and the Souls of Queer Folk

Emerging Perspectives in Pastoral Theology and Care

Series Editor
Kirk Bingaman, Fordham University

The field of pastoral care and counseling, and by extension pastoral theology, is presently at a crossroads, in urgent need of redefining itself for the age of postmodernity or even post-postmodernity. While there is, to be sure, a rich historical foundation upon which the field can build, it remains for contemporary scholars, educators, and practitioners to chart new directions for the present day and age. Emerging Perspectives in Pastoral Theology and Care seeks to meet this pressing need by inviting researchers in the field to address timely issues, such as the findings of contemplative neuroscience, the impact of technology on human development and wellness, mindfulness meditation practice for reducing anxiety, trauma viewed through the lens of positive psychology and resilience theory, clergy health and wellness, postmodern and multicultural pastoral care and counseling, and issues of race and class. The series will therefore serve as an important and foundational resource for years to come, guiding scholars and educators in the field in developing more contemporary models of theory and practice.

Titles in the Series

Christianity, LGBTQ Suicide, and the Souls of Queer Folk

Cody J. Sanders

LEXINGTON BOOKS
Lanham • Boulder • New York • London

Published by Lexington Books
An imprint of The Rowman & Littlefield Publishing Group, Inc.
4501 Forbes Boulevard, Suite 200, Lanham, Maryland 20706
www.rowman.com

6 Tinworth Street, London SE11 5AL, United Kingdom

British Library Cataloguing in Publication Information Available

Library of Congress Control Number: 2020932604

ISBN 978-1-7936-0609-9 (cloth : alk. paper)
ISBN 978-1-7936-0611-2 (pbk : alk. paper)
ISBN 978-1-7936-0610-5 (electronic)

∞™ The paper used in this publication meets the minimum requirements of American National Standard for Information Sciences Permanence of Paper for Printed Library Materials, ANSI/NISO Z39.48-1992.

To those queer souls for whom life, at times, seems unlivable

Contents

Acknowledgments

There is only one group of people for whom the statement, "this work would not have been possible without . . . ," is unequivocally applicable. This group of unparalleled importance to this project is comprised of the nine research participants who responded to my call for persons interested in participating in research on LGBTQ suicide and religion. If these nine individuals had not taken a flyer, sent an e-mail, answered a phone call, and then shown up at the appointed time to sit with me to engage in conversation about their lives, there would be no meaningful words with which to fill the following pages. If a *different* set of participants had volunteered to participate, the work that follows may have taken a different form. Thus, these *specific* nine people, in all of their particularity, have shaped my engagement with this important topic in meaningful and entirely unique ways. For this I am tremendously grateful.

A second group whose mentoring, support, and scholarly acumen influenced my formation as a pastoral theologian throughout the writing of the original iteration of this work is my dissertation committee at Brite Divinity School. Joretta Marshall, Nancy Ramsay, and Namsoon Kang graciously offered their keen theological insight to my emerging interest in this subject. Through their feedback, these three helped give significant shape to this dissertation where it was lacking. Their engaged curiosity in my developing research sent me in search of new pathways forward in the work when I felt that I was at a dead end. And their encouragement to transform this research into a publishable text was energizing. Through their friendship and support during the transitions of life throughout this writing, they have not just shaped and supported the production of a disembodied work of "scholarship." Instead, they have helped sustain my humanity.

I am thankful for my friends and colleagues whose friendship has nourished me through this weighty project, and whose thoughtful, scholarly conversation has made me a better pastoral theologian. These include past colleagues in the PhD program at Brite Divinity School, faculty colleagues who have supported the shaping of my research interests into courses I've taught at Andover Newton Theological School and Chicago Theological Seminary, and my clergy colleagues in Harvard Square who always express interest in my current writing projects. I am also grateful for the conversation and feedback on the original iteration of this work that I received from Avery Belyeu whose work in LGBTQ justice and suicide prevention is saving lives. I am thankful to Zachary Moon for the feedback I received on the chapter drafts as I transformed the research into the book you now hold. I am grateful for the support of my partner, Cody VanWinkle, as I worked on this manuscript (occasionally while we were on vacation). And I am appreciative for insightful feedback from the peer review I received on this manuscript in the publication process, and from my editors at Lexington Books.

Finally, I am thankful for the honor of receiving a Dissertation Fellowship from the Louisville Institute to fund the research and writing of this research project that began as my PhD dissertation. Moreover, that the Institute saw something of value in my work that they believed would meaningfully contribute to the study of religion and the promotion of vitality in American religious life buoyed my spirits throughout the process of research and writing.

Introduction

Stories give us life. And when life becomes unlivable, there are stories behind that too. For far too long, our religious narratives have contributed to the unlivability of life for LGBTQ people, resulting in suicide. This is the problem I take up in this book in search of a constructive response to the dangers that religious narrative pose to LGBTQ lives.

At its base, this book says something to us about what it means to be human in the midst of stories—to be human *because* of stories. We cannot understand ourselves without story. We cannot understand who we are in relation to the ultimate—God, Divine Presence, the Sacred, the Holy— without story. Our deepest sense of who we are, our connection to the communities in which our lives are deeply embedded, each of the cherished values and principles and truths that enliven our activity and animate our imaginations, our sense of place and significance in the cosmos—all of these are shaped by stories.

Some stories *we* tell. Some stories are told *about us*. Some stories swirl in the social consciousness long before we enter the world, punctuated by our birth, and catching us up in their narrative flow. We become a part of some stories without even knowing it, unwitting to how indelibly they shape our lives, our actions, our self-understanding. Arthur Frank argues that stories act as "the breath of god in creation stories, as that god gives life to the lump that will become human."[1] Stories give us life.

This book focuses on a critical juncture in the storied nature of our humanity: the *interruption* of life's narrative flow by an ambush of stories that make life seem unlivable. As Frank notes, "Sometimes, stories that have no place in people's inner library still teach those people who they can be; stories have a capacity for *narrative ambush*."[2] More precisely, this book is about the many ways that lesbian, gay, bisexual, transgender, and queer (LGBTQ) people experience the "narrative ambush" of religious, spiritual, and theological narratives that set life on edge, make life seem unlivable, and often lead to suicide.

As stories go, those that emerge from the sources we deem "religious" garner a great deal of power to shape lives and worlds. Even *naming* some stories as "religious" or "theological" or "spiritual" is a terminological shortcut to denote the power these stories exhibit in surviving the ages, circulating widely, shaping lives, creating worlds, and animating action that leads both to widespread generativity and healing, as well as destruction and death.

1

This book confronts the stark reality that many stories emerging from the ˙istian tradition have scripted and conscripted the lives of LGBTQ peop.   n ways that have led to our destruction and death. As gay Catholic theologian James Alison rightly says,

> For far too long, and it is not in any way surprising, gay and lesbian people have had to scrabble about for elements of story floating around, since the one story that was not available and open to us was the Christian one. The Christian story was specifically presented to us as one within which we could only inscribe ourselves by agreeing to mutilate our souls.[3]

The suicide of LGBTQ people is the most disturbing bodily materialization of this "mutilation" of queer souls.

In this book I address the role that religious, spiritual, and theological narratives play in shaping the souls of queer folk. Even beyond their explicitly religious content, there are ways that certain stories operate theologically by setting life within a presumed ultimate context, informing the "deep myths" that constitute a person's sense of "coreness"—those elements of our human experience we often point to with the metaphor of "soul."

SAVING THE SOUL

The word "soul" may seem a bit archaic. Many disciplines long ago interested in the purview of the soul have abandoned the concept in favor of more modern areas of inquiry like the "psyche" or "self." And often for good reason. As Larry Graham points out, many movements away from the soul are due to the "dualistic, spiritualistic, privatistic, and essentialist overtones" that the concept carries.[4] The soul has become anathema to both postmodern inquirers and to more scientific-minded scholars.

Philosophically, the rejection of mind/body dualism—that we are made up of two distinct parts: material body and immaterial soul—is clearly out of vogue. This view has happily given way to gradually seeing our "selves" as equally enfleshed and inspirited without the dichotomy of "body" and "soul" in opposition to one another. We are holistic creatures with no need to philosophically dismantle ourselves in order to understand each different "component" apart from every other.

Psychologically, the term "soul" was gradually replaced by other, more modern and "sophisticated" terms like "psyche," or "ego," or "self." As a "science of the soul," psychology largely outgrew its early metaphorical origins for more scientific-sounding terms that garnered psychologists greater credibility among those scientists for whom "soul" sounded much too pastoral and parochial. Aside from contemporary devotees of Carl Jung, very few psychologists or psychotherapists have much use for the term "soul" in their work of human healing.[5]

Religiously, talk of "soul" is tainted by long, embarrassing legacies of Christians on a crusade to *save the souls* of friends and foes alike, endeavoring to reach the world's multitudes whose souls, we believed, needed "saving" (sometimes at the point of a sword). Soul-talk among Christians is usually indicative of the corrosive religious one-upmanship that would place some souls on a lower plane in need of rescue by those "in the know," in closer relational proximity to the Divine, or on the "right side" of a cosmic religious battle of good over evil. LGBTQ people bore the brunt of this crusade in recent decades on the U.S. religious landscape.

Saving "soul" as a vital metaphor for this project is clearly a difficult task in light of this history. But for several reasons that will become apparent as the book progresses, I believe that soul is worth saving.

THE SOULS OF QUEER FOLK

The title of this book is an obvious allusion to W. E. B. Du Bois's famed text, *The Souls of Black Folk*. It was in my interview with a participant named Juliana that this connection was first made. Juliana, reflecting on the impact of Du Bois's book on her life as a young African American woman many years ago, said that it brought her "back to my sense of being an African American where we were for so long defined as not having souls to save." She saw this question as an important one in fighting against the white dominant discourse that suggested, "we have souls and they don't, so we can do anything to them that we want. Our souls are saved, their souls are not. We can do anything to them that we want. Kill them all, let God sort them out."

Du Bois writes, "It is a peculiar sensation, this double-consciousness, this sense of always looking at one's self through the eyes of others, of measuring one's soul by the tape of a world that looks on in amused contempt and pity."[6] And while the sociocultural and theological circumstances are different, Juliana and the other interview participants spoke to the question of "looking at one's self through the eyes of others" in ways that made the question of the queer "soul" pertinent in working against the heteronormative and cisgender dominant theological discourses by which LGBTQ people are so often expected to measure their own souls.

In brief, examining the ways that stories become dangerous to LGBTQ people for whom suicide becomes a thinkable option, I am interested in the helpfulness of "soul" as a useful *metaphor*—an *experience* that we may have of ourselves in the world, rather than an *entity* that we possess. Rather than the soul as part of the *nature of our being* (an ontological reality) or an always-and-already-there essence at the "depths" of our being (an essentialized reality), I'm developing the metaphor of soul to speak about our *sense* of ourselves as beings with an experience of "depth," as persons with a sense of mooring, grounding us and orienting us in relation to a presumed ultimate context. And this *sense* of our coreness develops from the stories and narratives that intersect our bodies to tell us something about who we are as human beings and how we are situated in the world in relation to this ultimate context.

Resisting modernism's drive to speak of a "reality" at the core of our ontology, I am interested in a *sense*, a *perception*, an *interpretive event* that may, at times, present in metaphorical terms as something that is "core" to who we are as human beings. In this iteration of the metaphor, we do not *have* a soul, but we experience a *sense* of "soul." We do not have a *core* to our humanness but we often experience a sense of *coreness*.[7] This is akin to the ways that Larry Graham defines "soul" as "a social reality that is always coming into being at new levels of organization, function, and value. It is ultimately never completed. It is a capacity, an achievement, and a discovery."[8] Narratives of "soul" traffic in the language of possibility: "could" and "if" and "maybe" and "perhaps."

In this book, the souls of queer folk come into view as a narratival event at the moments when the *coulds* and *ifs* and *maybes* and *prehapses* of the soul give way to an experience of precarity: when the narratives that take root in our storied soul threaten to uproot us, when our strongest moorings to ultimacy come unmoored, when our deepest sense of coreness begins to feel rotten to the core. It's in these cases that this book critically addresses the ways that the storied souls of queer folk can be ambushed by coercive sources of dominance that curtail freedom and make life difficult to live. The prevalence of suicide among LGBTQ people is a prime example of this death-dealing ambush of souls.

SUICIDE AND SOUL VIOLENCE

The suicide of lesbian, gay, bisexual, transgender, and queer persons has long lingered in social awareness—a reality that plays large in both literature and film.[9] The U.S. Surgeon General's 2012 National Strategy for Suicide Prevention names lesbian, gay, bisexual, and transgender populations as a group with increased suicide risk.[10] And in recent years, instances of LGBTQ suicide have come to more prominence in U.S. social awareness through intensified coverage of LGBTQ suicides in the mainstream news media.[11] While it's important to recognize that suicide is not ubiquitous among LGBTQ people—that there are many of us who live our entire lives never attempting or even contemplating suicide—it's clear that suicide is a reality of particular significance to those who are concerned for the wellbeing of LGBTQ people.

One meta-analysis of twenty-five studies that included data on 214,344 heterosexual and 11,971 non-heterosexual persons revealed a two-fold elevation in suicide attempts among lesbian, gay and bisexual persons when compared to the suicide rates of their heterosexual peers.[12] In the Surgeon General's report, all studies considered showed that 12 to 19 percent of lesbian, gay, and bisexual adults reported making a suicide attempt in comparison to less than 5 percent of all U.S. adults, while the numbers for adolescents is even more staggering, revealing at least 30 percent of LGBT adolescents reporting attempts compared with 8 to 10 percent of all adolescents.[13] While fewer studies have included transgender persons, the National Transgender Discrimination Survey reveals 41 percent of respondents (n=6,450) having reported a suicide attempt.[14]

While garnering the attention of professionals across disciplines, from medicine to public health to psychology, and frequently covered as a topic of public concern in the news media, the elevated occurrence of suicide attempts among LGBTQ persons has earned little attention within the literature of theology and religious studies.

When we consider what makes life seem unlivable for LGBTQ people who attempt or complete suicide, our metaphors matter. When we speak only in psychological metaphors of psyche or self, we tend toward a psychologization or medicalization of LGBTQ suicide. We make these experiences into indicators of "depression" or other psychopathologies, easily dismissing the complexities of the experience for LGBTQ people. While psychology and psychiatry hold valuable insight for helping us think about suicide among LGBTQ people, these literatures tend to overlook the nuance and critical significance of how religious beliefs, theological narratives, and spiritual practices affect the lives of LGBTQ people leading up to suicide attempt.

Where the social science data is effective in mapping the landscape of LGBTQ suicide, it falls short of fully exploring the religious and theological narratives that come into view in the stories of LGBTQ people who attempt suicide, and it offers little help in understanding how these narratives operate violently upon the souls of queer folk. If religious, spiritual, and theological narratives play a precarity-inducing role in constituting some LGBTQ people's sense of the core of experience their lives, the conceptual tools and metaphors of theology must be brought to bear in addressing the capacity for theological or spiritual violence against the souls of LGBTQ people.

CARE OF QUEER SOULS

Beyond an analysis of the research I've conducted with LGBTQ people who've attempted suicide and survived, I want to know: What can we do? How can we intervene in situations of narrative ambush—of soul violence—to cultivate life's livability?

Toward that aim, the book informs broad practices of care: the "care of queer souls." The chapters that follow will critically address the ways that stories, narratives, and discourses work to render some LGBTQ lives precarious, leading to suicide becoming a thinkable option. Approaching the concern of LGBTQ suicide in this way, with the old metaphor of soul and all of its problems and possibilities, will constructively shape the praxis of the "care of queer souls" that promotes possibilities for the livability and flourishing of life for LGBTQ people.

To do this, I spent time listening carefully to the lives of LGBTQ people who have attempted suicide. Through the process of research interviewing, I listen specifically to the voices of nine LGBTQ people for whom life at one time or another came to seem unlivable. These nine people spent time with me in the hopes that their stories might help other LGBTQ people in similar precarious situations. More than helping other individuals, though, many of these nine named their desire to help change the culture of religious communities in relation to LGBTQ lives as a primary motivation for participating in this research.

These are the nine whose stories and perspectives give shape to the material that follows. The participants real names are not used in the research. Instead, each of them chose a pseudonym by which they would be referred throughout the work, and you'll get to know their stories a bit more in the following chapter. They are my primary collaborators in this research and their words enliven this text in ways that no review of extant literature could.

Thomas is a forty-eight-year-old, White, cisgender man who identifies as gay. He grew up in a conservative Christian environment and continues to identify as Christian. Thomas is in search of a church in the mainline Protestant tradition that will embrace him as a gay man. Thomas was sixteen years old at the time of his first suicide attempt and age twenty-two at the time of his last attempt. He estimates that he attempted suicide from five to seven times over the course of that span of years.

Tandiwae is a is a forty-nine-year-old, White, cisgender woman who identifies as lesbian. She grew up Southern Baptist and also lists Pentecostal, nondenominational, and mainstream evangelical as other categories of religious and spiritual groups and practices with which she has identified over the course of time. Tandiwae was seventeen years old when she first attempted suicide and dates her last attempt at age thirty-seven.

Juliana is a forty-five-year-old, African American, cisgender woman who identifies as queer. Early in life, she grew up in the African Methodist Episcopal church and later became involved in "neo-Pentecostal" churches with her parents. Currently, she identifies as a non-theist Black Protestant. Juliana was thirty-three at the time of her first suicide attempt and identifies that as the singular attempt experienced in her lifetime.

Florence is a thirty-seven-year-old, White, cisgender woman who identifies as lesbian. She was raised in the Christian Reformed Church and is now a member of a liberal Protestant denomination and also practices Zen meditation. Florence was eighteen years old at the time of her first and only suicide attempt.

Silas is a forty-eight-year-old, Irish/Cherokee/Choctaw, gender queer person who identifies as a lesbian. Silas was raised Baptist in fundamentalist religious environments and now identifies as a "non-religionist." Silas was twenty-two years old when first attempting suicide and identifies that as a singular attempt.

Kate is a twenty-three-year-old, White, cisgender woman who identifies as a lesbian. While racially she identifies as White, she also identifies culturally as a third culture "islander," as she was raised outside of the cultural milieu of her parents heritage as the child of missionaries. She grew up Baptist and continues to identify as a "Reformed Baptist" — that is, a Baptist adhering to a Reformed theological framework. She was twenty-one-years old at the time of her first and only suicide attempt.

Matthew is a thirty-one-year-old, White, cisgender man who identifies as gay. He grew up Southern Baptist and is currently in process to join the Episcopal Church. Matthew was sixteen years old at the time of his first suicide attempt and twenty-nine at the time of his last attempt, having a total of four suicide attempts in that span of time.

Miguel is a thirty-year-old, Mexican/French, cisgender man who identifies as a "sexual being" in a same-sex relationship. He grew up in a nominally Catholic household and now identifies with "historical Christianity." Miguel was twelve years old at the time of his first suicide attempt and experienced a total of seven attempts, the last of which was at age fourteen.

Louise is a twenty-one-year-old, White, gender queer/pangender/fluid person of German/Irish heritage who identifies as pansexual. Louise described growing up in a "religiously religious" Catholic household. Louise now finds meaning in the spirituality of nature. Louise was sixteen years old at the time of her first suicide attempt and estimates that the last attempt was at age eighteen with two total lifetime attempts to date.

This is not a text about the "causes" of LGBTQ suicide, or a social scientific attempt to portray the statistical landscape of the phenomenon. In this text, I aim to honor the intentions of these nine LGBTQ souls when they agreed to participate in this research. They all voiced desires to aid other LGBTQ people for whom life, at times, becomes unlivable *and* to provide a constructive critique for congregations and communities of faith that are wittingly or unwittingly complicit in perpetuating the theological and spiritual narratives that set life on edge for so many LGBTQ people. Therefore, this book aims to expose the spiritually violent operations of theological narratives and develop constructive methods of contributing to the resistance and resilience of queer souls in relation to this soul violence.

Beyond description, this book has a pointed constructive aim: In listening carefully and critically for the souls of queer folks, I am in search of ˻ 'ance in reforming our religious practices in ways that promote the livab˷ ʃ of life for LGBTQ people. These nine individuals generously shared hours of their time with me, talking about some of the most difficult points in their lives—times when life seemed unlivable and they decided to end their own lives. In this book, I hope to honor these nine narratives in all of their difficulty and pain with an eye toward what we must learn from the souls of queer folk in order that life is more livable and *flourishing* is a better possibility than *death* for LGBTQ people. But the religious reform called for through these narratives will not only make life more livable for LGBTQ people. It will also help us to engage in a process of reforming religion, resisting soul violence, and developing practices of care that will make life more livable and religious practice more meaningful for all.

NOTES

1. Arthur W. Frank, *Letting Stories Breathe: A Socio-Narratology* (Chicago: University of Chicago, 2010), 3.

2. Frank, *Letting Stories Breathe*, 58.

3. James Alison, *Broken Hearts & New Creations: Intimations of a Great Reversal* (New York: Continuum, 2010), 49.

4. Larry Kent Graham, *Care of Persons, Care of Worlds: A Psychosystems Approach to Pastoral Care and Counseling* (Nashville: Abingdon, 1992), 42.

5. This has clearly not always been this case, as is noticeable in these titles from classic psychological theorists: Bruno Bettelheim, *Freud and Man's Soul* (New York: Vintage, 1982); Viktor E. Frankl, *The Doctor and the Soul: From Psychotherapy to Logotherapy*, trans. Richard Winston and Clara Winston (New York: Vintage, 1986); C. G. Jung, *Modern Man in Search of a Soul*, trans. W. S. Dell and Cary F. Baynes (New York: Harcourt, 1933); Otto Rank, *Psychology and the Soul: A Study of the Origin, Conceptual Evolution, and Nature of the Soul*, trans. Gregory C. Richter and E. James Lieberman (New York: Johns Hopkins, 1930/1998).

6. W. E. B. Du Bois, *The Souls of Black Folk* (New York: Penguin Books, 1903/2018), 7.

7. Similarly, James Ashbrook describes soul as a metaphor denoting *"the core of experienced reality."* James B. Ashbrook, "Soul: Its Meaning and Its Making," *Journal of Pastoral Care* 45, no. 2 (1991): 160.

8. Graham, *Care of Persons, Care of Worlds*, 42.

9. Larry Gross points to the fact that out of thirty-two films with major homosexual characters released between 1961 and 1976, thirteen of these films feature gay suicide. Larry Gross, "Out of the Mainstream: Sexual Minorities and the Mass Media," in *Gay People, Sex, and the Media*, eds. Michelle A. Wolf and Alfred P. Kielwasser (New York: Harrington Park Press, 1991), 28.

10. U.S. Department of Health and Human Services (HHS) Office of the Surgeon General and National Action Alliance for Suicide Prevention, *2012 National Strategy for Suicide Prevention: Goals and Objectives for Action* (Washington, D.C., 2012), 101.

11. This increased media coverage began to garner greatest attention in the months following the suicide of Tyler Clementi in September 2010, which took place amid a spate of gay teenage suicides related to school bullying.

12. Michael King, Joanna Semlyne, Sharon See Tai, Helen Killaspy, David Osborn, Dmitri Popelyuk, and Irwin Nazareth, "A Systematic Review of Mental Disorder, Suicide, and Deliberate Self Harm in Lesbian, Gay and Bisexual People," *BCM Psychiatry* 8, no. 70 (2008): 1.

13. U.S. Department of Health and Human Services, *2012 National Strategy*, 121.

14. Jaime M. Grant, Lisa A. Mottet, and Justin Tanis, *Injustice at Every Turn: A Report of the National Transgender Discrimination Survey* (Washington, D.C.: National Center for Transgender Equality and National Gay and Lesbian Task Force, 2011), 1.

ONE

God, Stories, and Queer Souls

Our deepest sense of who we are as persons, our connection to the wider communities in which our lives are embedded, each cherished value that enlivens our action in the world, even our understandings of our place and significance in the cosmos are all shaped by stories. Naming some stories as "religious" or "theological" or "mythical" is a linguistic way to denote the power these stories hold in their tenacious survival and life-shaping influence. Circulating widely across the ages, these stories shape individuals and communities, create worlds, and animate action that leads to widespread generativity and healing.

Religious stories also hold the power of destruction and death.

As Frank argues, "A good life requires living well with stories. When life goes badly, a story is often behind that too."[1] He goes on to say,

> Stories animate human life; that is their work. Stories work with people, for people, and always stories work *on* people, affecting what people are able to see as real, as possible, and as worth doing or best avoided . . . Human life depends on the stories we tell: the sense of self that those stories impart, the relationships constructed around shared stories, and the sense of purpose that stories both propose and foreclose.[2]

Many stories emerging from religious traditions have scripted and conscripted the lives of lesbian, gay, bisexual, transgender, and queer (LGBTQ) people in ways that have, at times, made life go quite badly.

There is no greater sign of life gone badly than when life comes to seem unlivable. Life's unlivability is a feature of lived experience that impinges upon LGBTQ lives at a much higher rate than that of straight and cisgender people. One way of framing that feature of lived experience is through statistics. Recall the Surgeon General's report, showing 12 to 19 percent of lesbian, gay, and bisexual adults making a suicide attempt in comparison to less than 5 percent of all U.S. adults, and at least 30 percent of LGB adolescents reporting attempts compared with 8 to 10 percent of all adolescents,[3] or the National Transgender Discrimination Survey's revelation that 41 percent of respondents (n=6,450) reported a suicide attempt.[4]

In taking LGBTQ suicide as a problematic site of lived experience demanding our urgent attention, my primary concern is what "work" religious, spiritual, and theological narratives perform on LGBTQ people leading to the point at which life comes to seem utterly unlivable. "A good life requires living well with stories. When life goes badly, a story is often behind that too."[5] What religious, spiritual, and theological stories are behind this immense statistical problem, and how do we effectively get at that granular level of experience to observe the power of these narratives to make life go badly for LGBTQ people? And, in turn, what work do LGBTQ people do *with* and *on* these narratives in order to resist their violent potential and enhance life's livability? These are the guiding questions of this book.

TOOLS FOR EXPLORING A COMPLEX RELATIONSHIP

Ideas, concepts, and theories operate like a box of tools to pick up and use on a problem. The hope is always to address the problem constructively, if not to "fix" it. But the tools you have determine the kind of work you're able to do on a given problem. For the problem of LGBTQ suicide, social scientists and psychotherapists have used the many conceptual tools in their well-developed toolbox—including statistical analysis of the problem—often to great constructive ends. The social science literature is, however, limited in its ability to address the intersection of religion and suicide in the lives of LGBTQ people.

In social science literature LGBTQ suicide is often framed as either a concern of healthy "identity formation," assessing the effects of stigmatization on LGBTQ youth, or a problem of "public health," assessing the emotional, social, and psychological factors of an "at-risk" group.[6] It is difficult to evaluate the complex intersection between LGBTQ suicide and religion within these frameworks. Typically, "religion" comes into view as just another potential source of stigmatization or a psychological stress factor for LGBTQ youth, but with little critical nuance or understanding of how these narratives do their work on LGBTQ people.

Further, the relationship between religion and LGBTQ people is a *complex* relationship. The relationship between LGBTQ people and religion cannot be wholly viewed as a risk factor contributing to suicide ideation. A more complete assessment of this complex intersection of LGBTQ people, religion, and suicide must also allow for ways of viewing religious and theological narratives' work on LGBTQ lives in "positive" or life-affirming directions as well. Such an assessment must also make room for viewing how LGBTQ people do their own work *on* damaging religious and spiritual narratives toward the livability of life. Even the statistical assessments of this complex intersection suggest the n⸱ for theoretical tools and conceptual frameworks that allow for such 1...anced inquiry.

In a 2018 article in the *American Journal of Preventative Medicine*, researchers attempted to understand the fraught relationship between LGBTQ people, religion, and suicide. Their hypothesis, not entirely supported by their findings, was that religiosity is *negatively* associated with suicide ideation and attempt for heterosexual people, but *positively* associated with suicide ideation and attempt for lesbian, gay, bisexual, and sexually questioning people. Rather than entirely clear correlations, however, the researchers discovered that "the association between religiosity and suicidal behaviors is complicated for LGBTQ individuals."[7]

The researchers concluded that the complexity of this three-way relationship and the lack of positive associations between religion and suicidality among *all* sexual minority groups may be the result of varied individual approaches to navigating these complex relationships—a complexity that the statistical picture is unable to portray. They suggest that "the heterogeneity in the results may speak to the potential nuanced ways that sexual minority communities navigate religious milieus."[8]

Yet, in the religious and theological disciplines, little to no work exists on the problem of LGBTQ suicide. Scholars in these disciplines have yet to bring their tools to bear on this critical concern. That is where my work picks up, drawing upon the tools of social science, philosophy, and theology to develop a constructive theological approach to the problem of religion and LGBTQ suicide. So, what conceptual and theoretical tools are needed to address the problems at the complex intersection of LGBTQ identities, religious and spiritual narratives, and suicide?

SOUL: A NARRATIVE METAPHOR

My contention throughout this work is that the conceptual metaphor, "soul," enables us to see more clearly—with greater nuance and complexity—the *work* that religious and spiritual narratives perform on LGBTQ people. As you might expect, "soul" has a long conceptual history.[9] It is impossible to see this long history of "soul" delivering to us a unified conceptual tool to bring to bear on the present question, so I am necessarily selective in my development and use of this tool. Largely, these choices hinge on the differences between "soul" as a metaphysical reality that we possess as an essence of our own being, and "soul" as a metaphoric term of ontology. In this vein Edward Findlay argues, "It is with a fundamental ontology, not a metaphysics, that this conception of the soul can be understood. To understand the soul in this sense one must not think of it as an entity, a thing, but as the locus of our relationship to our own being." [10] As an ontological metaphor—pointing us toward *the locus of our relationship to our own being*—how can "soul" help us to see the work that religious discourse performs on LGBTQ lives leading to suicidality?

A Sense of "Coreness"

In a scientific and psychologized era, "soul" can seem an overly parochial and pastoral term. We now generally traffic in the language of "psyche" or "self" to talk about our sense of who we are as human beings. I am not suggesting that those terms be abandoned as conceptual tools for working on the problem of LGBTQ suicide and religion. But these conceptual tools of our scientific and psychologized era do little to help us get at the complex and nuanced ways religious and spiritual narratives do their work on us *differently* than other narrative sources.

In this work, I am interested in how "soul" can help us look at certain aspects of our relationship to our own being with more critical nuance. James Ashbrook suggests that "soul" serves as a helpful conceptual metaphor when we understand it as a metaphor for "coreness," arguing that "soul is less a thing than *the core of experienced reality*" [11] referring "to core and characteristic ways people experience and express reality." [12] In other words, I am developing the conceptual tool "soul" not as an entity that we possess but an *experience* that we have of ourselves in the world—an experience of our own "coreness."

Rather than an essentialized "reality" always and already there, resting in the "depths" of our being, a *sense* of our coreness points to the ways stories and narratives constitute our "deepest" awareness of who we are as human beings. The metaphor reveals operations of religious power and theological knowledge intersecting our bodies to produce a perceptual *experience*—a narrative *sense*—about who we are as human beings and how we are situated in the world. In other words, resisting an essential "reality" at the core of our ontology, I am interested in "soul" as a *sense*, a *perception*, an *interpretive event* that, at times, presents in metaphorical terms as something that is "core" to who we are as human beings.

In this iteration of the metaphor, we do not *have* a soul at our "core," but we have a *sense* of "soul" that feels, at times, something like our "core." In my work with LGBTQ research participants who share their narratives of life coming to seem unlivable leading up to attempting suicide, I am looking for a *sense* of coreness that participants experience that I can meaningfully address and assess with "soul" as an ontological metaphor for our relationship to our own being at the core of who we are as humans.

Meaning-Making Souls

Not an essence, but a sense. Our sense of our own coreness—the locus of our relationship to our own being—is formed and reformed through the "work" that stories perform on us. And this work is a meaning-making function in relation to our experiences of our body and being in the world. Gordon Kaufman argues,

> The *distinctiveness* of the human over against other forms of life increasingly impressed itself on men and women. As a way of understanding and interpreting this distinctiveness, they developed religious and philosophical conceptions of the *soul*, a distinct nonmaterial kind of reality taken to be the very heart of our humanness. [13]

At the "heart of our humanness" is a meaning-making function that we can locate within the ontological metaphor of soul. We make meaning of many things—perhaps *every* "thing" that we encounter—but when we make meaning of *our own distinctiveness* at the locus of our relationship to our own being, this meaning-making function is indicative of the site of inquiry I am interested in here: the site I am calling "soul."

This meaning-making function of soul operates in several ways. Herbert Anderson equates soul with the function of making meaningful memory by linking past and present, cultivating a history and a continuity of identity. [14] Charles Gerkin similarly names his perspective on this function of soul, arguing, "The life of the soul is a continuous life of interpretation." [15] Gerkin says this hermeneutical, meaning-making, interpretative life of the soul is a "profoundly social process," embedding souls in an ecology of meaning and language that is shared with others in historically situated contexts. [16]

At the heart of the questions raised by the complex intersection of LGBTQ lives, religion, and suicide, there is an interpretative, meaning-making process at work, situated in the "ecology of meaning and language" that is shared with family, faith communities, and the larger social context in which the research participants are embedded. Our interpretative, meaning-making locus of our relationship to our own being cannot be adequately assessed without understanding the entanglement of religious narratives in larger social contexts doing their work on the sense of coreness of LGBTQ souls.

Soul as Contextualized Activity and Outcome

As part of an ecology of meaning-making situated in our social contexts, Larry Graham interprets the metaphor of "soul" in a psychosystems perspective that I continue to develop in my own use of the metaphor. Graham argues,

> When applied to the human personality or psyche, the concepts of
> systemic thinking reveal the human self as a relatively open system
> rather than as autonomous and nonsocial. The soul is both the *activity*
> of synthesizing and creating experiences, and the *outcome* of the pro-
> cess of synthesis and creation."[17]

As an *activity*, the soul is a receptive process of influencing and being
influenced by the multiple systems in which an individual is embedded.
As an *outcome*, the soul is what "results" from this process and is formed
over time by the contextualized work that narratives perform on us.[18]
Graham continues to move us away from fixed essences to dynamic
senses, saying, "The soul must rather be thought of as a social reality that
is always coming into being at new levels of organization, function, and
value. It is ultimately never completed. It is a capacity, an achievement,
and a discovery."[19]

The dynamic contextualization of activity and outcome—coming into
being with a sense of coreness—is especially relevant to assessing and
addressing the complex intersection of religion and LGBTQ suicide. The
conceptual tool of "soul" as I develop it here helps us to see the narrative
"work" being done on LGBTQ people by religious stories, and the agential work that LGBTQ people reciprocally perform in relation to these
narratives within their social contexts. There are no one-way relationships between narratives and souls. Soul is a dynamic, open-ended coming-into-being—an activity and an emerging outcome.

Even when social factors like isolation, rejection, stigma, etc. are
named in the social science literature as risk factors negatively affecting
the identity development of LGBTQ persons, the focus often remains on
the *effects* of these social factors upon the individual, rather than the
dynamic nature of the social construction of queer souls as an activity
and outcome, or a coming-into-being. Charles Taylor similarly argues
that, often, however tightly the dependence of the individual upon which
the social is conceived, "it is seen in causal terms, and not as touching our
very identity."[20] The "causal" assessment in much of the social science
literature is limited in assessing the narratival work being performed on
the coreness of our identity within the dynamic social contexts in which
we are embedded, especially when it comes to our embeddedness with
religious traditions and communities.

A few social science researchers, however, do point us toward the
more social, reciprocal, and contextual understandings that I am developing here. Michel Dorais, for example, argues that suicide among LGBTQ
persons is best construed as a *social* phenomenon, rather than a purely
personal or individual act. This, he explains, is due to the fact that while a
person enacts suicide individually, "the individual who attempts it or the
one who completes the attempt does not act in isolation from other contexts and motives stemming from life experiences that are social and have

a history."[21] I use the conceptual tool of "soul" to offer an assessment of the interpretative, meaning-making activity occurring at the intersection of religion and LGBTQ lives that sometimes leads to suicide attempt through a process that intimately links the individual with their social context. This is narrative "work" that is not "causal" but touches our very identity.

Embodied Souls

When it comes to suicide, we cannot treat souls and bodies as dichotomous, separate entities. It is largely the "dualistic, spiritualistic, privatistic, and essentialist overtones" that Larry Graham argues are the primary reasons many in contemporary theological scholarship have abandoned use of the metaphor of "soul."[22] Soul has too often been placed in opposition to body.

Yet our conceptions of "soul" have long imagined the seat of the soul within some bodily locale. Donald Capps picks up on the metaphorical relation of "soul" with particular bodily locations and their respective characteristics such as the regenerative possibilities of the liver in ancient Greek thought about soul.[23] Other theorists and theologians interested in the neurological basis for the soul metaphor have argued that "soul" is best seen as "a semantically designated portion of the soul-mind-body whole."[24]

I aim to close the gap between body and soul in ways that position the metaphor "soul" as closely related to bodily experience. Shawn Copeland argues, "For the body is no mere object—*already-out-there-now*—with which we are confronted: always the body is with us, inseparable from us, *is* us. But, always, there is a 'more' to you, a 'more' to me: the body mediates that 'more' and makes visible what cannot be seen."[25] It is this "more" that my use of soul attempts to address, while maintaining that this "more" cannot be entirely distinct from the body as the locus and mediator of the "more." This points us to a conceptual soul rooted in the flow of one's experience, particularly one's *bodily* experience related to a person's sense of sexual and gender identity. Looking for the soul in the narratives of LGBTQ suicide invites us to ask what interpretive, meaning-making work is happening at the level of our relationship with our own being, with the body fully in view as an integral, mediating aspect of our being.

Storied Souls

As is clear by now, my use of the metaphor of "soul" in this work has a decidedly narrative frame. But if we view the entirety of our sense of self, or identity, as a socially constructed, narratival creation, what use is there for a specific locus of narratival coming-into-being that we name "soul"? Gerkin is again helpful here in stating, "The self's story has about it an aura of a deep myth that images the way things are and should be for that self. Thus the self's story may be seen as the soul's myth of the self in the world."[26] He continues,

> Self stories may frequently be found to express in more hidden ways an ultimate level of assumed atmosphere that reveals the individual's perceptions of the final context in which the life of the soul takes place. For some that atmosphere is assumed to be fundamentally friendly toward the self...For others the final climate of things is more over against the self's intentions or indifferent to the struggles of the soul.[27]

It is this "aura of deep myth," this "ultimate level of assumed atmosphere," this "final context," that is my interest in looking at the lives of LGBTQ people through the metaphorical lens and conceptual framework of "soul." Some of the most pertinent instances of this aura of deep myth for this study will be the points at which the "final climate of things" interrupts the narrative progression of the self's intentions and the soul's struggle.

We can view all of life and our sense of self in the world as constructed by the work of language, narrative, and discourse but still fail to see the ways that different narratives do their work on us *differently* because of the contexts from which those narratives arise and the (ultimate) contexts of which those narratives purport to speak. As a conceptual "tool" to pick up in this work and use on the problem of LGBTQ suicide, soul as a narrative metaphor invites a closer examination of the ways LGBTQ people for whom suicide becomes a thinkable option are being "worked on" by religious and spiritual narratives—developing understandings about how these narratives are "affecting what people are able to see as real, as possible, and as worth doing or best avoided."[28]

To summarize: as I search for the soul at the complex intersection of religion, suicide, and LGBTQ lives, what I am looking for are the narratives that express a *sense* of a person's coreness, speaking to the locus of their relationship with their own being. I am looking for the interpretative, meaning-making activity that occurs as a social process, allowing a window into the outcome of religious and spiritual narratives' "work" on people. I assume that this activity is dynamic, always working toward a coming-into-being that speaks to the "more" of our bodily experience in the world, but always relates to the body and its corporeal experience. More often than not, this narratival sense will look something like an aura of deep myth about a persons' assumed atmosphere in which they live and move and sense the core of their being, speaking to a final or ultimate context for understanding their self in the world. This area of inquiry is what I point to with the metaphor of "soul."

RELIGIOUS AND SPIRITUAL NARRATIVES

With "soul" now developed as a narrative conceptual tool of inquiry, how do religious and spiritual narratives perform their "work" on us? What avenues into the exploration of the complex intersection of r ̣ion and LGBTQ suicide does "soul" offer? What stories, narratives, ̣ ̣d discourses are operating theologically in ways that set life within a presumed ultimate context and inform the "deep myths" that constitute a person's sense of "coreness," constructing the locus of their relationship with their own being? And how does this narrative "work" contribute to the possibility of suicide becoming a thinkable option for LGBTQ people?

The following chapters are all responses to these critical questions, drawing upon the narratives of LGBTQ people who have attempted suicide and survived. But before delving into the complexities of those stories in search of the ways religious narratives are doing their work on the souls of queer folk, it is important to understand what narratives are deemed "religious" or "spiritual" for the purposes of this study, and how those narratives will be assessed for their "work" on queer souls.

Stories, Narratives, Inner & Collective Libraries

While we often use the terms "story" and "narrative" interchangeably, there are ways that seeing these two terms differently may prove useful for our purposes here. Frank defines stories as *actors* in human consciousness—sometimes acting in ways the individual is aware, and other times acting outside of an individual's conscious awareness. "People have often forgotten the stories that think in them," Frank says.[29] His method for understanding the ways that stories "think in us" is called "socio-narratology" and I take up many of this analytic tools in my approach to the complex intersection of suicide, religion, and LGBTQ lives. Socio-narratology's two axioms in understanding the "work" that stories perform on us are these: (1) no individual ever thinks a story that is entirely original, and (2) no individual thinks a story alone.[30]

While stories act in individual human consciousness, "*Narratives* are the resources from which people construct the stories they tell and the intelligibility of stories they hear."[31] Frank argues that the action of stories is constrained by a number of narrative templates, saying, "Stories in any field can and often do draw on more than one template, but the templates are the fundamental narrative resources that set the terms of thinking, acting, and even imagining in their field."[32] To understand how stories and narratives operate in human lives, Frank draws upon the metaphors of "inner" and "collective libraries" from the work of French literary theorist and psychoanalyst Pierre Bayard. Bayard, explains his concept of "collective library," saying,

> Most statements about a book are not about the book itself, despite
> appearances, but about the larger set of books on which our culture
> depends at the moment. It is that set, which I shall henceforth refer to
> as the *collective library*, that truly matters, since it is our mastery of this
> ɔllective library that is at stake in all discussion about books. But this
> ʃtery is a command of relations, not of any book in isolation.[33]

The collective library might aptly be understood as framing the ways that
larger socio-cultural narrative templates construct the telling and the intelligibility of the stories that operate within the individual human consciousness.

Bayard explains the corollary concept of "inner library" as "that set of
books—a subset of the collective library—around which every personality is constructed, and which then shapes each person's individual relationship to books and to other people."[34] While Bayard is speaking of
actual *books* as literary influences upon an apprehension of the world,
Frank adopts this book/library language as a metaphor for thinking about
how stories and narratives (that are *not* literal books) also populate individuals' self-understanding and apprehension of the world.

Frank furthers Bayard's concept of inner and collective libraries by
augmenting "habitus," a central concept in the work of French sociologist
Pierre Bourdieu, to fit a narrative frame, arriving upon the concept of
"narrative habitus." Frank posits, "In simplest terms, the inner library is
the organization of narrative habitus; less simply, it is the dynamic principle by which stories have their effects."[35] Narrative habitus is by far the
most important methodological tool that I use in this research to understand the work of religious and spiritual narratives upon queer souls.
This is the concept by which we will come to understand the ways that
religious and spiritual narratives "do their work" upon queer souls leading to suicide attempt.

Narrative Habitus

In Frank's perspective, the concept of "narrative habitus" is as close as
we get to the concept of "soul" as I have developed it above. What is
missing from his purview, however, are the ways that religious, spiritual,
and theological narratives organize the narrative habitus—how these
narratives become something of an "aura of deep myth" by which we
live and die. Nevertheless, narrative habitus is a critical conceptual tool
for the purview of this study, augmented by a theological approach to the
concept.

Frank expands the concept of "narrative habitus" by asking "why . . .
people take up the identities they are called to assume?" One's narrative
habitus is "the collection of stories in which life is formed and that continue to shape lives."[36] This collection of formational stories disposes one to
listen to some stories more attentively than others, repeating some stories

more frequently than others.[37] Thus, while it may be commonsensical that some stories of self-understanding are more pronounced in the construction of one's self-understanding, an examination of narrative habitus asks what stories within the *inner library* and what connections to narratives in the *collective library* dispose one to attending more carefully to some soul-shaping stories while ignoring others.

Frank describes the structure of narrative habitus in four stages. First, narrative habitus speaks to a repertoire of stories that an individual recognizes as operative within the social group(s) to which the individual belongs. As the following chapters explore, the cultural, familial, and religious context of the LGBTQ participants in this research contain a repertoire of stories that these individuals had available to draw upon to make sense of life—particularly, ways of making sense of their sexuality or gender identity in relation to their religious upbringing.

Secondly, narrative habitus contains one's competence to use this repertoire of stories as embodied knowledge for apprehending reality and constructing a sense of self. This becomes important not only when assessing the ways that LGBTQ persons drawn upon religious narratives to shape their own sense of coreness leading to a suicide attempt, but also in addressing the ways that these same persons work with these stories in order to become competent theologians toward the livability of life after one or a series of failed suicide attempts. The narratives of these nine queer souls demonstrate an incredible competence to use the religious narratives operative within their religious social group in order to resist their violent outworking on their souls.

Thirdly, Frank says that narrative habitus disposes a person's tastes for some stories over others, holding profound implications for which future stories an individual will be open to.[38] One of the most surprising elements of the research which will become evident later are the ways that participants held closely certain religious, spiritual, and theological meaning-making narratives in the aftermath of a suicide attempt, even amid the clear perception of how similar narratives had made life go quite poorly leading up to the attempt. Their disposition toward these religious narratives populating their narrative habitus, however, seem to contribute to their continued use of these narratives in making possible other futures beyond suicide.

And finally, narrative habitus predisposes individuals to a sense of "right and fitting" resolutions toward which stories should progress, providing a feeling about what move should come next in a narrative progression.[39] This is an important part of assessing the narrative habitus and its connection to the soul's aura of deep myth when it comes to suicide attempt among LGBTQ people. As the following chapters make evident, for nearly every participant there were clear reasons why suicide was assessed as the next "right and fitting" resolution toward which their story progressed. Without an understanding of how religious, spiritual, and theological narratives lead to suicide as the next step in a narrative progression, it is difficult to critically assess the ways these narratives do their work on queer souls. Similarly, without attending to the agential ways that LGBTQ people do their own work on these elements of their narrative habitus, one misses an important part of why suicide didn't become the final resolution toward which their stories progressed. The soul's sense of "right and fitting" narrative progressions is amenable to resistance and change.

In this research, I aim to employ the concept of narrative habitus to understand the ways that stories and narratives make a claim upon the lives of LGBTQ persons, what these stories and narratives are, and how they gain prominence in an individual's narrative habitus leading to "next narrative moves" that include the contemplation and enactment of suicide. Though the narrative metaphor is prominent in this research, we cannot forget, as Frank reminds us, that "stories compel because they express in narrative form what begins in bodies."[40] Or, stated another way, "*Narrative habitus* is the embedding of stories in bodies."[41]

Rather than the straightforward "data" of facts and sequential story-telling, the research participants whose narratives enter this book in the next chapter act as *organizers of narrative* speaking to the meaning made of experience, rather than relating bare "facts" of a sequential story.[42] Attending to this organization of narrative is key to understanding a narrative habitus that makes some narratival movements and future stories more tenable than others. Holstein and Gubrium explain, "Pursuing this image of the interview metaphorically, the storyteller is not reading from a fixed text; he or she is improvising, speaking to the interactional and informational challenges of the immediate circumstances."[43]

Thus, the "data" I am rendering from interviews with research participants is not the supposed "raw facts" of experience, but narratives by which the participant "activates and manages" meaning related to the experience of LGBTQ suicide—particularly dimensions of this experience that might be termed "religious" or "spiritual."[44]

Parker notes that such an examination of narrative's influence on lives "brings us closer to an examination of how discourse functions ideologically, how it presents an oppressive version of the world that may feel suffocating to speakers and listeners, and which shows no way out."[45] These "oppressive" and "suffocating" presentations of the world and the ways in which they function ideologically in rendering life unlivable will be of primary importance to me in the analysis of interviews.

Theo-Narratology

Connecting his understandings of stories "breathing" to the "breath of god" in creation stories, Frank argues, "Socio-narratology . . . analyzes how stories breathe as they animate, assemble, entertain, and enlighten, and also deceive and divide people."[46] This breathing, animating, assembling quality of stories and narratives is the basis for my use of socio-narratology as an appropriate methodological tool for this study. When applied to the conceptual metaphor of "soul" as defined above, however, this socio-narratology shifts toward a "theo-narratology" in my attention to the aura of deep myth about a persons' assumed atmosphere in which they live and move and sense the core of their being, speaking to a final or ultimate context for understanding self in the world—a context often labeled with the term "God."

What sets theo-narratology apart from *socio*-narratology, as developed by Frank, is an inquiry into how the stories and the narratival resources are *performing theologically*. That is, how are the narratives purporting to position human beings and the world in relation to "God"—or at least the word "God"[47]—forming the "deep myths" that are constitutive of a person's sense of coreness? And, how does the narrative placement of human lives into a presumed "ultimate context" through theologically laden narratives shape the livability of lives, opening the possibilities for both flourishing and subjective precarity, leading to suffocating and oppressive presentations of the world and to the cultivation of breathing space and methods of resistance?

One's narrative habitus disposes one to listen to some stories more attentively than others, repeating some stories more frequently than others.[48] *Theological* narratives make an especially potent claim upon the identities people are called to assume—*intensifying* the process through which narratives form our sense of coreness by setting these narratives on a transcendent horizon. Freeman illuminated the importance of this horizon of meaning, saying,

> One might therefore speak, cautiously, of the *transcendent horizon* of the life story, by which I refer to those dimensions of the life story that are, finally, about the state and destiny of one's very soul . . . [that] appear to refer to ideals that transcend societal norms and expectations and point toward images of fulfillment and completion that are difficult to contain within a purely immanent framework . . . [providing] a horizon of ultimate meaning and value that conditions the very judgments that can be made about right and wrong, good and bad.[49]

While colloquially, it seems that a "religious" or "spiritual" narrative should have explicitly "religious" or "spiritual" content—saying something about the doctrine or teachings of a religious or spiritual tradition—this is not always the case in my treatment of narratives as "theological" in this book. More than their content alone, some stories and narratives—even ones without explicit religious content—still *operate* theologically, setting life within a presumed ultimate context and informing the "deep myths" that constitute our sense of "coreness." Likewise, some very explicitly religious narratives, purporting to disseminate particular religious doctrines, may very well *fail* to operate theologically by speaking to a final or ultimate context for understanding self in the world. Even narratives without explicitly theological content may still meaningfully be called "theological" when the symbol, "God," is taken to represent one's concerns with ultimacy, not necessarily specifically *deity*.[50]

Additionally, this theo-narratological inquiry will attempt to curtail the ways that certain narratives—some of which are thought of as "theological" and others falling outside this construction—can tend toward "finalizing stories" and rendering other perspectives silenced.[51] I am interested in theology as an "'imaginative construction' of a comprehensive and coherent picture of humanity in a world under God"[52] and the ways narratival frameworks contribute to these imaginative constructions and to the formation of a narrative habitus out of which a person lives and/or dies.

Thus, rather than theological narratives and sources occupying a distinct content, narratives must be examined for their potential to imaginatively set life "in a world under God" or within a presumed ultimate context that isn't always necessarily "theologically" languaged but that still holds potential to profoundly shape a construal of "reality" and possibilities for life, thusly *operating* or *functioning* theologically and amenable to the vantage point of a theological perspective or standpoint of research.

Frank names the intention behind this type of analysis, stating, "The objective of hermeneutic interpretation is not to display mastery over the story, but rather to expand the listener's openness to how much the story is saying."[53] A theo-narratological method is particularly interested in what the story might be saying about a person's sense of how one's life is set within a presumed ultimate context, or in relation to "God."

Drawing upon the metaphor of soul, Charles Gerkin helpfully addresses this level of analysis, stating, "Self stories may frequently be found to express in more hidden ways an ultimate level of assumed atmosphere that reveals the individual's perceptions of the final context in which the life of the soul takes place."[54] I understand Gerkin here indicating a *function* of narrative that we may aptly term "theological." Theological attentiveness to this narrative function of setting life in a presumed "ultimate context" is a way of drawing upon, while moving beyond, socio-narratology through expanding an openness to just "how much the story is saying" and what effects the story has upon the livability of life.

Here, "soul" is a useful metaphor for pointing toward the "more" that is constructed by social discourse, imported into our narrative habitus and enfleshed, inextricably, in the corporeal body and bodily experiences. Suicide is, of course, one such bodily experience through which the "more" of social and theological discourse is enfleshed. In this framework, we can understand suicide as an embodied outcome of what Frank names as a sense of "right and fitting" resolutions toward which an individual's stories should progress—providing a feeling about what move should come next in a narrative progression.[55]

Finally, it should be clear by now that part of my impetus to reclaim and re-vision "soul" as a vital metaphor for understanding LGBTQ suicide is to say that there is more to being human than can be exp᠁ ᠁ned and explored by scientific discourse—social scientific or otherwi᠁᠁. Soul is a term with a conceptual history that pushes us to continue a search for non-commodifiable understandings of our humanity—our values, aspirations, and sense of place in the world in relation to others and in relation to an ultimate context. The theological understandings and practices developed in the aftermath of suicide attempt, employed in resistance to narratives that operate violently upon the soul, will provide a direction I will pursue in the final chapters toward undertaking the praxis of care for queer souls in a narratival, intersubjective mode.

NOTES

1. Arthur W. Frank, *Letting Stories Breathe: A Socio-Narratology* (Chicago: University of Chicago, 2010), 3.

2. Frank, *Letting Stories Breathe*, 3.

3. U.S. Department of Health and Human Services, *2012 National Strategy*, 121.

4. Jaime M. Grant, Lisa A. Mottet, and Justin Tanis, *Injustice at Every Turn: A Report of the National Transgender Discrimination Survey* (Washington, D.C.: National Center for Transgender Equality and National Gay and Lesbian Task Force, 2011), 1.

5. Frank, *Letting Stories Breathe*, 3.

6. Maralee Mayberry, "The Story of a Salt Lake City Gay-Straight Alliance: Identity Work and LGBT Youth," *Journal of Gay & Lesbian Issues in Education* 4, no. 1 (2006): 14.

7. Megan C. Lytle, John. R. Blosnich, Susan M. De Luca, and Chris Brownson, "Association of Religiosity with Sexual Minority Suicide Ideation and Attempt," *American Journal of Preventive Medicine* 54, no. 5 (2018): 645.

8. Lytle, Blosnich, De Luca, and Brownson, "Association of Religiosity with Sexual Minority Suicide Ideation and Attempt," 649.

9. Raymond Martin and John Barresi, *The Rise and Fall of Soul and Self: An Intellectual History of Personal Identity* (New York: Columbia University Press, 2006); Stewart Goetz and Charles Taliaferro, *A Brief History of the Soul* (Malden, MA: Wiley-Blackwell, 2011).

10. Edward F. Findlay, *Caring for the Soul in a Postmodern Age: Politics and Phenomenology in the Though of Jan Patočka* (Albany, NY: State University of New York Press, 2002), 63.

11. James B. Ashbrook, "Soul: Its Meaning and Its Making," *Journal of Pastoral Care* 45, no. 2 (1991): 160. Emphasis in original.

12. James B. Ashbrook, *Minding the Soul: Pastoral Counseling as Remembering* (Minneapolis: Fortress, 1996), 169.

13. Gordon D. Kaufman, *In Face of Mystery: A Constructive Theology* (Cambridge: Harvard University Press, 1993), 107. Emphasis in original.

14. Herbert Anderson, "The Recovery of Soul," in *The Treasure of Earthen Vessels: Explorations in Theological Anthropology*, eds. Brian H. Childs and David W. Waanders (Louisville: Westminster John Knox Press, 1994), 211.

15. Charles V. Gerkin, *The Living Human Document: Re-Visioning Pastoral Counseling in a Hermeneutical Mode* (Nashville: Abingdon, 1984), 104.

16. Gerkin, *The Living Human Document*, 110.

17. Larry Kent Graham, *Care of Persons, Care of Worlds: A Psychosystems Approach to Pastoral Care and Counseling* (Nashville: Abingdon, 1992), 42. Emphasis in original.

18. Graham, *Care of Persons, Care of Worlds*, 42.

1 ˀraham, *Care of Persons, Care of Worlds*, 42.

2 ˀarles Taylor, *Human Agency and Language: Philosophical Papers 1* (New York: Camu   ;e University Press, 1985), 8.

21. Michel Dorais, *Dead Boys Can't Dance: Sexual Orientation, Masculinity, and Suicide*, with Simon L. Lajeunesse, trans. Pierre Tremblay (Montreal & Kingston: McGill-Queen's University Press, 2004), 15.

22. Graham, *Care of Persons, Care of Worlds*, 42.

23. Donald Capps, "The Soul as the 'Coreness' of the Self," in *The Treasure of Earthen Vessels: Explorations in Theological Anthropology*, eds. Brian H. Childs and David W. Waanders (Louisville: Westminster John Knox Press, 1994), 97.

24. Warren S. Brown, "Cognitive Contributions to Soul," in *Whatever Happened to the Soul? Scientific and Theological Portraits of Human Nature*, eds. Warren S. Brown, Nancey Murphy, and H. Newton Malony (Minneapolis: Fortress Press, 1998), 102.

25. M. Shawn Copeland, *Enfleshing Freedom: Body, Race, and Being* (Minneapolis: Fortress, 2010), 7.

26. Gerkin, *The Living Human Document*, 112.

27. Gerkin, *The Living Human Document*, 114.

28. Frank, *Letting Stories Breathe*, 3.

29. Frank, *Letting Stories Breathe*, 14.

30. Frank, *Letting Stories Breathe*, 14.

31. Frank, *Letting Stories Breathe*, 14.

32. Frank, *Letting Stories Breathe*, 123.

33. Pierre Bayard, *How to Talk About Books You Haven't Read*, trans. Jeffrey Mehlman (New York: Bloomsbury, 2007), 12

34. Bayard, *How to Talk About Books You Haven't Read*, 72–73.

35. Frank, *Letting Stories Breathe*, 54.

36. Frank, *Letting Stories Breathe*, 49.

37. Frank, *Letting Stories Breathe*, 53.

38. Frank, *Letting Stories Breathe*, 53.

39. Frank, *Letting Stories Breathe*, 54.

40. Frank, *Letting Stories Breathe*, 81.

41. Frank, *Letting Stories Breathe*, 52.

42. James A. Holstein and Jaber F. Gubrium. *The Active Interview* (Thousand Oaks, CA: SAGE, 1995), 19.

43. Holstein and Gubrium, *The Active Interview*, 28.

44. Holstein and Gubrium, *The Active Interview*, 31.

45. Ian Parker, *Qualitative Psychology: Introducing Radical Research* (New York: Open University Press, 2005), 90.

46. Frank, *Letting Stories Breathe*, 16.

47. This question accords with Gordon Kaufman's argument, saying, "Theology, however, is not so much devotion to the symbols of faith as the attempt to *understand* those symbols and the way they function in human life, to criticize and reinterpret them so they will more adequately achieve their purpose, and finally . . . to reconstruct them, sometimes radically . . . it is particularly sensitive to difficulties or problems in the formulation and implications of those symbols. It is a *deliberate human activity* directed toward criticizing and reconstructing the symbols by which faith lives and to which faith responds." Gordon D. Kaufman, *An Essay on Theological Method*, 3rd ed. (Atlanta, GA: Scholars Press, 1995), xx.

48. Frank, *Letting Stories Breathe*, 53.

49. Mark Freeman, *Hindsight: The Promise and Peril of Looking Backward* (New York: Oxford University Press, 2010), 94.

50. For example, Cooper-Lewter and Mitchell make the argument, "A world view that functions as a basis for emotional balance must be recognized as theology." See Nicholas Cooper-Lewter and Henry H. Mitchell, *Soul Theology: The Heart of American Black Culture* (Nashville, TN: Abingdon, 1991), 6.

51. In narrative's potential to teach persons "who they can be," narratives can come to operate in a "finalizing" manner, presenting a sense of narratival "wholeness" no longer allowing narratival construction to proliferate. See Frank, *Letting Stories Breathe*, 58, 103. In contrast, "Dialogical analysis has little interest in excluding—it welcomes a proliferation of possibilities, which confirms that the story or stories can never be finalized" (110). Narratives that tend to operate in a "finalizing" manner present ideas beyond which we cannot go, simply because we yet have no words to surpass them. But when uttered with metaphysical-foundationalist presuppositions regarding our ability to name the really Real or what is True about nature, ourselves, the world, or the Divine, we suppose that these linguistic devices tell us something of an "ultimate context." It is the ability of certain narratives to operate in these ways—whether or not they are overtly "theological" or "religious" in content—that become the focus of a theo-narratology.

52. Kaufman, *An Essay on Theological Method*, ix.

53. Frank, *Letting Stories Breathe*, 88.

54. Gerkin, *The Living Human Document*, 114.

55. Frank, *Letting Stories Breathe*, 54.

TWO

Troubled Stories, Best Hopes, Precarious Survival

The research I present in the following chapters emerges from many hours of recorded interviews I conducted with nine participants. These nine volunteered for the research out of their willingness to speak with me about the intersections of their sexual or gender identity, their religious lives, and their suicide experience. Most of them did with the hope that their stories would provide some aide to other LGBTQ people in similar situations. And many also voiced a desire to help *churches* to become safer, more life-giving places for LGBTQ people as well.

In the chapters to come, I put these narratives into conversation with the literature of philosophy, theology, psychology, and varied other disciplines in order to identify themes that hold potential to shape practices of care in relation to LGBTQ lives. But before I begin extracting pieces of these lengthy interviews for critical examination, I believe it is important for readers to get to know these nine participants in a fuller sense than interview excerpts can provide.

Ann Lowenhaupt Tsing says of stories, "we need to tell and tell until all our stories of death and near-death and gratuitous life are standing with us to face the challenges of the present. It is in listening to that cacophony of troubled stories that we might encounter our best hopes for precarious survival."[1] That is my hope in rendering these nine individuals' stories here. And that, too, was *their* hope when they first told their stories to me.

THOMAS

Thomas, forty-eight-years-old when we spoke, "wrestled" all his life with being gay and Christian. His father was a lay Unitarian minister and his uncles were also ministers. His paternal grandfather achieved only a fourth-grade education, but read the Bible exhaustively. This familial background typifies Thomas's experience of religion as a child. "I sang in church when I was three years old. I believed in Christ from like a small boy and I wanted to be a minister since I was age six," he explained.

Thomas spoke of his adolescence in this atmosphere, saying, "I would participate in youth groups as best I could and feel these attractions for the other boys and know that one of the most powerful aspects of who I was was absolutely forbidden in any social circle in the community. So I stayed alone with it. I kept my faith in Christ. I always have." He began drinking at age fifteen and taking drugs in college partially to deal with the sexual abuse he experienced as a ten-year-old at the hands of an older boy, and partially to deal with the growing "distance" he sensed between himself, the world, and the grace of God.

By the time he was in college, Thomas had "let the whole church thing go" and attempted suicide first at age sixteen and several other times after that. He described, "going out into the car and closing the garage door and turning on the car and leaving it on. Just when I was going to pass out I'd turn it off and open the door and think . . . I didn't know why I wanted to live but I didn't know why I wanted to die." Thomas also attempted overdosing on drugs on a couple of occasions. Once, after taking two hits of acid, Thomas recounts his most vivid attempt to end his life, saying,

> I became convinced on that day that the reality was that God was going to take everybody up and this was going to be hell . . . because there was something wrong with me. So I ran into this building and I ran up the stairs and a friend ran after me. I got to the top of the stairwell and I climbed over the railing and he pulled me back. And I threw him to the ground and wrestled him and I pinned him until he stopped struggling. He was okay, but he stopped struggling and let go of me. Then I climbed back over the stairwell. And I was praying the whole time, it was only prayer, just over and over again: "God, save me." And I jumped off. And I inverted and I dropped about twenty feet, maybe a little more, and I landed on my face on concrete steps. And I didn't pass out. I didn't break bones. My nose hurt a little bit. I have no idea why I survived that.

All throughout these attempts at suicide, even after having left regular church attendance behind, Thomas described showing up periodically at various services. Once, at a little church near the airport on the outside of town, he responded to an altar call when he heard a voice inside him saying, "Go up and pray." At this church, he sensed that God didn't want him to be gay or to drink or take drugs, so he stopped. He promptly broke up with his first boyfriend he had ever had and joined a Christian ministry on his college campus.

Thomas, who describes himself as "a marrying kind of guy," began dating a woman he had known since high school. "So she knew I had been gay and we both believed firmly—*firmly*—that if we had the right kind of faith we could make me straight," he explained. So th' got engaged. His mother took his wife-to-be aside and told her that ' .iomas was gay. "He won't be after he gets married," his fiancée assured her. So they were married. Thomas got drunk at the reception so that he couldn't drive them to the honeymoon hotel and he continued drinking all through the honeymoon.

He was accepted into a PhD program in another city, but once he arrived in town to begin classes, he had the sense that something "had broken within [him] and it couldn't be fixed." Within two weeks of beginning doctoral courses, he couldn't continue. His wife was upset. "She started hitting me because I couldn't be the man she wanted, I guess. She was angry with me and I didn't understand. And I was committed, you know, like when you get married, *you get married*." So they began having children. But when the abuse continued Thomas threatened to kill his wife if she didn't stop hitting him. So they ended their marriage and he left.

After leaving his wife and children and the PhD program, Thomas sought therapy and psychotropic medications. Nothing helped. But he entered Alcoholics Anonymous and became sober. "I started reading the Bible exhaustively . . . I would read chapters of it and then I would meditate and I would go for walks. I became like a monk," Thomas says. "I withdrew from all my friends who partied and everything. And I became somebody else and then I couldn't find a way back . . . I couldn't get over the feeling that there was something really really wrong with me being gay."

"So, I basically stayed alone. I had my faith and that's all I had."

TANDIWAE

One of the strongest iterations of a sense of Christian vocation coming into conflict with one's sexual identity was voiced by Tandiwae, a forty-nine-year-old, White, cisgender woman who identifies as lesbian.

"I knew as a young kid that, you know, four years old I'm realizing there's something different about me," Tandiwae says. And from as early as she can remember, she was regularly in church. Raised Southern Baptist in the "deep south," it took Tandiwae a while to realize that her father was a preacher because *most* people she knew, like her own family, were heavily involved in church.

At the same time that her family's religious tradition was becoming so important to Tandiwae's identity as a child, she also began sensing an emerging attraction to women.

"I realized at that time that I wanted to be close to women and not men . . . And I thought, 'Hmm, this is interesting, this is strange.' So when I look back, I realize that's when I knew I was a lesbian without knowing th͏ ʌnd so I stayed secluded as I grew up." But it was in junior high schͻ   hat Tandiwae says, "life really changed for me and I realized, whoa, I am different."

She soon started attending a youth group at another church in town. "That youth program [is where] I really realized that I really did like girls. And I still didn't know what the word was, but I'm being called 'fag' and 'weirdo' and 'creepy' and all that stuff," she explains. Bullying and teasing was combined with messages she perceived as condemnatory toward same-sex attraction that she heard in sermons. She says, "Sitting there and listening to all the sermons all the way through high school, sometimes they would just pointblank tell you that it was wrong to be something that you shouldn't be." But the messages were often subtle.

> The preachers never said the word "gay" when I was growing up. But it was like an underlying thing because I don't remember ever having the gay issue such a strong thing as it is now. And maybe it's because I'm listening now. But at that time, I didn't understand it all and I certainly wasn't going to act on it. I certainly wasn't going to show that I was acting on it. Or at least try — try to hide it as best as I could.

So Tandiwae struggled with her emerging sense of sexuality in silence. "And I knew that I could not ever act upon my liking another woman. It was just something that would have to stay hidden within me," Tandiwae explains. "But I also knew that my dad's teaching and what we were learning in Sunday school was that we're all God's children, we're all loved, but there is a certain distinction between men and women." Yet, at the very same time, she vividly recalls the contrasting message preached from the pulpit, "you are going to die and go to hell if you do anything outside of the boundaries." Though these messages *didn't* come from her father's pulpit. She explains,

> I do not ever remember my father preaching those from the pulpit. And I asked him later on when he retired, I said, "Dad, how come you never preached upon these things?" And he said, "One, I didn't understand it, so I can't preach on something I don't understand. And two, I just wanted to preach about the Gospel of Jesus Christ." And that was his true aspect. He wanted to tell everybody that Jesus loves them. And that was his theology. But it was a very strong theology. And . . . as he got older and I came out to him . . . he actually wrote a letter to the Southern Baptist Convention, that they needed to change their theolo-

gy . . . and they needed to start preaching about the love of Jesus and accepting all people and to stop condemning and they needed to educate, not indoctrinate.

But coming out to her larger Christian community was not as positive for Tandiwae. At one point, she worked at a Southern Baptist camp in a job that she found greatly fulfilling. During the summer Tandiwae befriended a woman in town known by the camp employees to be lesbian. While their friendship was strictly platonic, Tandiwae was told she had to stop hanging around this lesbian woman if she wanted to keep her job at the camp. This was the first episode she recalled of her faith community forbidding a fulfilling relationship with another person because of sexual orientation and it sent a clear message to Tandiwae, who wasn't yet open about her own sexuality.

She recalled the painful episode of later coming out to her community the year that she met her partner.

> I came out to myself two years earlier than that, but still didn't know how to come out. I was, "Ok, yes I am gay. Ok, yes I need help. Ok, yes I need to work through these issues." And I was still involved in the church. And as soon as I came out openly, I was booted from every church I was involved in, which to me, was devastating. Because that's all I knew, that's all I thought I was worthy of because that's how I had been brought up.

Amid such theological messages of condemnation and communal acts of rejection, Tandiwae recalls her early suicidal ideations. Tandiwae traced attempts to harm herself in various ways and her contemplation of enacting suicide in a way that would cause the least pain possible to her family all the way back to age twelve. "We lived in an area where there was nobody around," she explains. "So I would throw myself up against a tree. I would smack my hands in the lockers after school when nobody's around. And I would sit there and pound my head and just wish that I would just like cause an aneurism or something and I'd be done. Or I would break my neck and I'd be done. You know, it'd be freak accident."

As she got older, she says, "I remember driving down the road and I'd be in some zone and I would have no idea where I just drove through. Because I was thinking about, 'Man, if the next diesel comes by, I'm going to just pull right in front of it and life [will] be done.'" She continues,

> Or I would look at the embankment I knew was coming around this corner and what if I just keep flying and, you know, say that my pedal got stuck, maybe they'll just think my pedal got stuck or something and I'll just fly off this ridge. Nobody will ever miss me. And then I would stop and think, what would that do to my mother? That would freak my mother out and she's already a basket case anyway. What would that do to my father's ministry . . . ? Everything kept bringing

me back so I never followed through but I'd get really close to it. I mean, I would slam on the breaks and pull over and just weep. "What am I doing? Why can't you deal with this?" So it became a "why can't *I* deal with it?" I brought it back to me. Because that's what you're taught. It's your problem, your fault. Then I would sit and say, "God, why did you make me this way? God, why can't I change? God, why can't you heal me? God, why can't you fix me? Why am I this way? Can't you change my thinking? You're supposed to be able to do all these things." And then I would get frustrated.

She was pulled on one side by theological messages condemning her sexual self-understanding, and on another by a strong sense of call toward a vocation in ministry—each narrative pull emerging through closely related theological narratives. Tandiwae summed up her dilemma with these words:

I knew, as a gay woman—openly gay woman—that I would not be able to do the music ministry that I wanted to do, that I would not be able to work in the churches and with people and with kids that I wanted to do because then I'd be considered a molester. I did know that word and I did know that gay people couldn't do any kind of church-affiliated work, which was the only thing I really believed that I ever was supposed to do or could do—work with ministry. That was it.

SILAS

Silas is a forty-eight-year-old Irish/Cherokee/Choctaw gender queer person who identifies as a lesbian. She grew up in a fundamentalist Baptist environment and attended a fundamentalist Christian university. This is where the majority of her storytelling centered. She says, "I liked being at [the University]. I liked the spiritual elements, I liked the people, I liked the academics, the environment—everything was nice, I mean, it was good, you know." Already aware of her same-sex attraction as a student at the university, Silas had hoped that something would change for her or that she would meet a mate, believing that the university would be "a good place to find somebody." As hopeful as she was that something might change for her in this new environment, she harbored a great deal of suspicion:

You know, thinking I would change but also knowing that I wouldn't. You know, that being gay is as inherent as, you know, our skin, our everything that we're made of. Having those feelings, you could suppress them. And I have over the years. But it doesn't change, you know, it's still a part of who we are. It's an inherent part of being a person.

While she was home for the summer before her senior year of college, Silas had a romantic encounter with another woman. It was, in her words, "a minor experience," but one that she wrote about in her journal. When she went back to the university, her roommate read her journal and made copies of it and took the pages regarding her same-sex romantic experience to the school's Dean of Women. She explains,

> I had to go to the Dean of Women's office and they asked me whether I considered myself to be homosexual. I answered the question that, "Yes, while I had those feelings and they were a part of who I am, that I did. But, while I was there and I wasn't really doing anything about it while I was there, no." So they sent me out of their office and they brought me back in and they said, "We're going to let you graduate but we're going to change you to a different room. We're going to send all your journals home to your mother."

But the school also stripped her of her campus ministerial responsibilities as a chaplain and a prayer captain—roles that were meaningful to Silas as an emerging ministerial leader.

After that, folks would talk about her behind her back as she walked across campus. Then one day her dorm supervisor called her into her office and asked Silas, "Knowing what you know about yourself, do you think you should stay here?" Silas thought about the question and answered honestly, "Knowing what I know about myself, no. I don't think I should stay." Because, as Silas admitted, "that was against their rules and I was coming to terms with [the fact that] it was a part of me and . . . I had one close friend that we were practically in love with each other, except that we couldn't be." So she left the university and moved back home to work part-time at a newspaper with a gay friend she knew from high school.

Silas found community in gay bars near her home because it was one of the few places she knew to meet other gay and lesbian people. "We didn't have the Internet. We didn't have any gay churches that I knew of." But she also admits that it would have been difficult for her to go to a "gay church" because of her own religious perspectives. She explains,

> So if there was like a Universalist church, a Unitarian church, when I would go there it just wouldn't align with my philosophies. So I had a hard time. What I wanted, I guess, was my cake and eat it too. I wanted to be able to have the religion and beliefs and thoughts that we had, and I had, and I wanted to be able to marry the woman of my choice.

In fact, there was a woman at her university that she dreamed of marrying. That dream included both of them becoming missionaries in Latin America because they both spoke Spanish and were deeply religiously committed. "But," Silas said with some pain, "that wasn't going to happen because her mom was praying for her to have a car and a husband and she got both and that worked out fine."

Silas's mother had difficulties with same-sex attraction. "She loved men and was attracted to men and she couldn't understand people being gay," Silas said.

> One day she was getting ready for work, and it must have been my day off. And we got into some kind of discussion and we were face-to-face I remember in the hallway at her house. And somehow she asked me or I told her that I was gay, and when I did she didn't like it and she punched me in the face. My mom's a tough woman.

When her mother went to work, Silas decided to kill herself. She found a bottle of lithium that her stepfather took for a mental illness. "I took I don't know how many—as many as I could," she said. "And I went to lie down in my bed and I thought I would just die and that would be the end of it."

But then she began having second thoughts. She remembered a family member who had a medical condition that left her comatose and Silas began imagining herself in that situation. She had visions of being "a person just lying in bed having to be taken care of because she died, she *almost* died but not quite." So she dialed 911 and was taken to the hospital. Fortunately, the only damage was minor harm to her kidneys. Her aunt came to pick her up from the hospital to stay with her and later her mother came to the house and apologized. After that, much changed for her mother and she began going to gay bars with Silas and having fun with her friends.

Yet, for Silas, the hope of becoming straight still lingered. "I met a nice man and we started dating and then I got engaged and I was engaged for a couple of years. But then I thought, 'Why am I playing this role? That's not who I am.'" And she called off the engagement. She explained her dilemma, saying, "each time it's like I kept trying to do one or the other. I tried to fit the expectations. And then I just tried to be myself. And it just was that pendulum back and forth." Explaining her grappling with the religious narratives related to her sexuality, Silas said,

> I've always felt and believed that God never leaves us and, you know, we have a lot of the truths God gives us regardless of how we are sometimes. You know, God still will be there, but you know, you also have verses like, "The way of the transgressor is hard," or whatever. So I thought, here I am, I'm just nothing but a transgressor, always going to be seen that way, so I guess I'm just going to have a hard life and I just kind of went with it.

FLORENCE

Florence, a thirty-seven-year-old, White, cisgender woman who identifies as lesbian, was brought up in a relatively conservative denomination in the Reformed tradition. Family and religion were vital parts of her life growing up. Her parents instilled in her from an early age that it was important to ask questions about faith and religion and when she went off to college, she began exploring other churches within the wider Christian tradition and continued to immerse herself in artistic engagement as she had throughout her childhood.

When it came to homosexuality, Florence's operative understanding from her growing up years was encapsulated in the phrase, "love the sinner, hate the sin." The appropriate way to respond to gay and lesbian people as she understood it was "to love them as human beings but to disparage what they do and who they are."

I had talked to my guidance counselor at school and said that I was having these feelings for my best friend who was a woman and he kind of said, "Well, you know, everybody sort of goes through these kind of phases and it's probably just something that you're going through and its totally natural. Just don't act on it because that would be bad. But you'll get through it."

At the time, this message felt liberating, allowing Florence to feel the feelings she was experiencing believing that they would someday pass. She said,

> I really sort of took to heart what my guidance counselors said and thought that this was maybe just something I was going through and that I would grow out of it. And I had mostly had boyfriends in high school and I really liked them. It wasn't hard for me. There wasn't a conflict there. It wasn't like I was pretending. So I just kind of figured this is an anomaly and something that I'll grow out of and it'll be okay as long as long as I didn't do anything. For me it was like, as long as I didn't act on it, I wasn't complicit or I wasn't doing anything wrong as long as I wasn't sort of actively engaged in anything.

She later talked with her pastor about her feelings of same-sex attraction, receiving the message from him, "Unless you're really sure, don't tell anybody because it'll just make your life really hard," and recommend that she seek counseling, perhaps from an ex-gay ministry like Exodus International. She declined to do so.

But as Florence met more out gay and lesbian people in college, she began challenging the rhetoric she had been exposed to regarding homosexuality and began asking what she really wanted in her life. When she realized that what she really wanted was a romantic relationship with another woman, Florence experienced a crisis. Florence experienced her only suicide attempt in college during a process of coming to an understanding of herself as lesbian. This occurred "somewhere around coming into knowing who I was and thinking about how I wanted to be in the world and all of the conflict that kind of comes with that," Florence stated. She describes this conflict, saying,

So I was interested in thinking about what that would look like and I had absolutely no idea how to reconcile it with my faith. I really thought I was going to become an atheist. And that almost terrified me almost as much as being a lesbian—the sense that I would have to give up Christianity.

LOUISE

Lou.   a twenty-one-year-old, White, gender queer/pangender/fluid person of German/Irish heritage, identifies as pansexual. She grew up in a Catholic family—"religiously religious," as she describes them. She dealt with a number of stressful situations in her growing up years. She says her family was "kind of falling apart," she wasn't doing well in school, she suffered from insomnia and would often be too tired to attend school, and she dealt with persistent bullying in school—"just the general bullshit essentially," as she names it.

Her family went to church every Sunday and Louise was baptized as a baby in the Catholic Church. "I definitely consider myself the black sheep of that family," she said, "because even as a child, I never really, like, I just didn't feel welcome in the community." Her family moved many times during her growing up years and she was part of several churches.

She vividly recalls one priest she encountered in one congregation who she describes as "pretty liberal and pretty progressive," and he was the only person that she ever remembers talking about gender or sexuality in a positive way in church. Aside from that priest, everything else she heard about sexuality—heterosexual sexuality or otherwise—was "overwhelmingly negative." She describes the nature of religious discourse in her family, saying,

> I mean the comments that come out of, like, my dad's side of the family—out of their mouths—is just sometimes unbearable to hear because it's so painfully negative. And even if it wasn't affecting me as a child before I understood my sexuality and I really was struggling with it—like as a young, young child—even then I felt like, it just felt painful to me. It was hard to hear. And I can't really—even to this day—can't really articulate exactly what was going through my mind.

So Louise only stayed in church for a brief time and curtailed the opinions she wanted to express to her family. She explains, "It was just so stressful to be around that environment because I was constantly double-checking everything I say and do all the time."

She was sexually active with her male peers at a young age. "I felt like I was trying to like reinforce myself. Like, reinforce my sexuality and being feminine and like, you know, whatever—attractive to males and things," she explains. She also reported being sexually abused by a girl seven years older when Louise was only six or seven years old. She believes that was a major factor in her avoidance of dealing with her attraction to other women. "I'm just really nervous around women," she says, "and so that kind of hindered me exploring my sexuality."

As she got more and more involved in sexual activity with men, she felt that she was reinforcing a delusion of her sexuality and gender existing in binary terms. "I just felt like I was trying to hard to be something that I wasn't, basically. Which was an over-feminine girl . . . And I wasn't happy and I didn't feel like myself." She continued, "I was still in that chaos phase and I was over sexualizing myself to make up for the guilt that I felt for being so lost and confused."

She had her first sexual experience with another woman at seventeen or eighteen and began at that point identifying as bisexual, before more recently shifting toward "gender queer," "pangender," and "pansexual" as identifiers when she started to recognize that a person's sex wasn't a central factor in her attraction to them, and that gender, more broadly, is a social construct.

Her attempts to understand her sexuality and to challenge the sexuality-shaming discourse that surrounded her in her church and her family growing up were not proving successful. She explains,

> The fact that I, I don't know it was, like, even though I knew that out loud I could say, "This isn't dirty. This is just normal. This is biology," whatever. Out loud, you know, I could rationalize it. But I was still dealing with that, like, "This is wrong." Even though it isn't, like, it's wrong and it's dirty and it's something that you don't talk about. I never had the sex talk with my family. Like, they never had that talk with me. And I felt guilty about being on birth control. You know, just every little thing, every little aspect in my daily life was like, I felt guilty about.

She identifies her first suicide attempt as stemming from a place of anger and resentment—some of which related to her religious upbringing. She ingested sleeping pills and attempted to drown herself in her bathtub, but felt guilty because she didn't want her mother to have to find her dead and aborted the attempt.

Her second suicide attempt emerged more from a place of guilt. "Guilt upon guilt upon guilt," she described it. Years of various influences enforcing the sense of guilt led to feelings of guilt over her sadness, even guilt for wanting to die. And Louise couldn't locate any supportive person to share these feeling with. She explained, "And so when I was going through the hardest points in my life when I felt like I had no friends or nobody I could rely on, I couldn't even go to my family. And that was what was so hard. Like, you're suppose to have one thing to fall back on and I didn't have that one thing, it felt like."

JULIANA

Juliana is a forty-five-year-old, African American, cisgender woman who identifies as queer. Twelve years went into her suicide attempt, she says, speaking thirteen years on the other side of surviving the attempt to end her life. She continues,

> I mean, I've tried to figure out was it twelve years that went into it or was it my whole life that went into it? That's why I answered that one question the way I did because you think you have a handle on it, you think you have a narrative around it and then things happen and you have to change that narrative.

Juliana grew up in a predominantly African American denomination and both of her parents were pastors. She attended a religious college that she describes as a "cauldron" of "politically right wing, theologically conservative . . . center of evangelicalism." She explains her impetus to attend that school: "The idea was to go there and, because they believe in supernatural healing and whatever ails you believe and you will receive it, etcetera, etcetera. So, I knew what I was going for. I was going to be healed of my homosexuality." She described the decision further, saying, "Every time I run, I run right into this. So I came to the one place where I thought I could be just, you know, that's it. I come here and I get my healing and that's it."

She had been "conditioned" in her growing up years that there was something wrong with her that "needs to be excised." Looking back on her college choice, she reflected, "Being in an environment . . . where you're just inundated with that and it was on purpose—I did it on purpose." But, she said as she laughed, "one of the things that I found there is that I was not alone in going there for that reason."

And yet, Juliana describes here experience with religion as a 60/40 split—60 percent negative and 40 percent positive.

> And so when you're left with a big forty percent like that you have to say, well, what part of it—you know, to have an integrated self—I can say, ok well, these terrible things happened to me and I can blame religion. Or I can say, all of these things happened in part because of religion and so what do I do now? So what do *I* do?

It was in college that Juliana first revealed her same-sex attraction, and by the beginning of her third year in school, she fell for a female TA who "seduced" her. Juliana described her decision to enter a relationship with her, saying, "The more I run from this the more I run smack into it. So I'm going to do an experiment. I'm going to stop running. I'm going to, quote, 'give in.'"

"But the deeper issue," she explained, "was that I'm going to actually question what I've been told." This was the issue that was of most concern to her parents. She described what she told them with these words:

> I said, "You don't control my thoughts. You don't control my beliefs. You don't control anything about me." And that's hard for a preacher's kid to do . . . Well when both of your parents are pastors and they have the legitimacy that you do not, just as a young person and as a person who is daring to question them. You really do feel like you're out on a limb. It's meant to be an isolating experience. It's one of the things that keeps you in the fold. It's the fear of being alone or being on your own or can't make it with out them. Then you start to realize, well I'm twenty years old, what do you mean I can't make it without them?

And the following summer, her parents kicked her out of the house over her sexuality, her questioning of her religious tradition and her parents' authority, "over all of it." While she hadn't yet disclosed her sexual attraction to other women to her parents, they told her "God had told them that I was on my way to being a practicing homosexual." That, she says, began what she sees as the twelve-years that led up to her suicide attempt.

When they confronted her with their suspicion, Juliana confirmed what they suspected and admitted to being in a relationship with another woman, which led to a "violent confrontation." Her parents beat her up over the course of an entire weekend. They confiscated her journals and threatened to expose the TA with whom she had been in a relationship. And at the end of the weekend, they made her leave the home. She spent several week sin a women's shelter and then found a place of her own in another city. She took a year off from college and devoted her efforts to getting back into school as an independent student, which she eventually did. "It just gets tiring. It gets tiring . . . I was just tired. I was really tired," Juliana says

She had few people in her life who could understand the complexity of her experience—few people, she says, "who are willing to take the time to hear what you're saying, whatever it is that you're saying." Out of the complexities of her experience, in the aftermath of a love interest that had gone "very badly" and a lot of alcohol consumption, she cut her wrists in order to bleed to death. She described the sense of "futility" that led to that moment:

> That futility that you—this is all, yes, this is all there is. This is it. This is all you get. And what you've gotten, Juliana, is a very mixed bag. You have gotten a mixed bag. So you can't cover it up with books. You can't cover it up with the pursuit of knowledge. You can't cover it up. This is it. So that futility that I think had gone on, I mean, definitely since [college] days, thinking, yeah, the more I run, the more I'm going to run smack into it. That basically took over.

But her attempt to end her life ended without her death. The very fact that she could not successfully carry out her own suicide was a turning point in her experience. She explained,

> I just cut myself but I was at a point where I wasn't even thinking clear enough that as soon as you cut yourself your body's going to start healing whether you want it to or not. So where you get this idea that you're just going to bleed to death, I mean, I still don't know where I got that idea from. Total fantasy, just complete fantasy. But then you see it happening. You see the blood coagulating and you're like, I still can't get out of here. Okay, so what am I going to do now? So being confronted with something as simple as that can be, I mean, it's jarring but it's also it helps you realize what you think about yourself isn't necessarily true. It's not necessarily so . . . You don't have as much control as you think you might, not even over your own existence.

She concluded her reflections upon her suicide and her mother's death and the years she spent caring for her father in the midst of his declining health and eventual death, saying, "So the sense of, I guess, the sense of self that comes from that is people can withstand a lot. I guess I'm one of them."

MATTHEW

Matthew is a thirty-one-year-old, White, cisgender man who identifies as gay. He grew up Southern Baptist and at the time of the interview was in process to join the Episcopal Church. Matthew's family went to a Southern Baptist church for the first eight or nine years of his life but then ceased attending church altogether. Matthew, however, began attending church with friends who went to one of the largest churches in his state—also a Southern Baptist congregation.

When Matthew was eighteen, he began to realize that he was gay and slowly stopped going to church. Yet he decided to attend a Southern Baptist college for his freshman year. He soon recognized that his emerging sense of sexuality could put him at odds with his college, resulting in expulsion if the revelation of his sexuality came to light on campus. He reported,

> I know for a fact that there were other gay people at [the Baptist college], but they were in the closet, you know. I'd hear reports of, you know, if students at [the college] when to [the local gay bar] that the University would send out spies to keep track of who they saw go in there and would report it back to the administration and those students would either get very heavy sanctions or be completely expelled from the University.

Thus, Matthew made the decision after his first year of college to transfer to a public university where this possibility would no longer be of concern.

Even at his new public university, Matthew attempted to retain his religious practices and communities through involvement in the Baptist Student Union and Campus Crusade for Christ. Eventually, however, Matthew reports, "I got so frustrated with religion and how they treated gay people that I dropped out." At that point, the university's gay student group was the only organization in which he retained involvement.

It was during college that Matthew made two attempts to end his life. His last attempt Matthew doesn't connect to his sexual identity, but to his diagnosis of obsessive compulsive disorder and the difficulty he had dealing with that diagnosis at work and in his life more broadly. His first suicide attempt, however, Matthew describes as "directly religiously involved" with a number of other factors that also went into the decision.

Matthew was bullied at school for his weight, for not being masculine enough, for not being into sports, and the ways he was perceived to fall short of a masculine ideal. He attempted to date a girl during this time and once they broke up, Matthew felt guilty for dating her, knowing that he was not attracted to women. He continued striving to live up to the expectations of his church, saying, "I guess up until I was, like, eighteen and twenty I tried to be, you know, the perfect Christian or whatever. Didn't drink, didn't smoke, didn't have premarital sex." This became more and more difficult during college when Matthew's same-sex attracting and Christian identification came into greater conflict.

A few of Matthew's friends who knew of his emerging sense of same-sex attraction convinced him to go to an ex-gay ministry to rid himself of homosexuality. Attending this ministry, he reports, "kind of messed me up and just got me feeling bleak." He believed that if he didn't keep going to this ex-gay ministry that he would lose the friends who sent him there. Matthew spent approximately three years attending two different ex-gay ministries—one in his home city and one near his university.

Matthew said, "I guess for like a couple of years during my early part of college I really struggled with, you know, knowing my attraction to men, but wanting to be Christian at the same time and not feeling I could be both." He continued,

> It made me feel like I was a disappointment to my friends at church and a disappointment to God. Like, that something was really, that I felt like I had a birth defect or something. That I wasn't, that made me just want to be normal like all the other people around me . . . I tried to talk to my youth minister at [my church] and, you know, he just encouraged me to keep going to the ex-gay ministry and avoid people that might cause me, lead me into temptation as far as, like, avoiding other gay people and stuff like that.

He very soon realized, however, that his sexuality wasn't going to change.

Speaking about the teaching concerning homosexuality instilled in him throughout his life before he had the tools to critically reflect on those teachings, Matthew said, "I wasn't able to think for myself. And once I was able to do that, I was able to start lifting some of the depression and other feelings of guilt that I've dealt with."

> I came to realize that it wasn't God that was causing my problems with Christianity, it was people that I was going to church with and, you know, certain denominations' practices. And it really took a while around here. Because it's only been the last several years that more gay affirming churches have started popping up in this area . . . And until I found our about some of the more open and affirming churches in the area, I just, you know, I would read my Bible at home.

After college, Matthew's longing for a religious community led him to Unitarian Universalism and then—desiring a more explicitly Christian church—Matthew began the process of joining the Episcopal Church. Near the end of his interview, Matthew reflected back on his story, saying, "I personally take the signs of me still being alive as a fact that God was looking out for me and didn't want, you know, didn't think it was my time to go yet."

KATE

Kate is a twenty-three-year-old, White, cisgender woman who identifies as a lesbian. While racially she identifies as White, she also identifies culturally as a third culture "islander," as she was raised outside of the cultural milieu of her parents heritage as the child of missionaries.

Growing up with conservative Christian missionary parents, same-sex attraction and sexuality were presented to Kate growing up as something that was "always sin, wrong, and never really any room for question." She had heard many stories and read statistics about people coming out to parents or confessing their "struggles" with same-sex attraction that made her afraid of the results of talking to her own parents about her sexuality. It was, she said, as if homosexuality was the "sin-of-all-sins" as she understood it. She recounted one family story that instilled in her this notion when she overheard a conversation her grandfather was having with other family members:

> My grandfather was talking about these two guys that he worked with, I guess they were in a relationship or something like that, and he was saying that he would have gotten his shotgun out and taken care of it, and that kind of thing. So those kinds of things, it was like it would scare me and make me think, okay, well maybe that's what Christian

people and, I don't know, maybe that's what my family—maybe all of them—think that way.

For these reasons, Kate kept her sexuality a secret from her family until years later.

She attended a fundamentalist Christian university and encountered other situations that exacerbated her felt need for hiddenness. She says, "I think maybe if I hadn't been [at the University] I probably would have maybe been more open about my sexuality and tried to get help. But I think being there—I had friends that had been kicked out for being gay." She opened up to a roommate a bit, but that, too, didn't go well and it instilled in Kate a sense of fear if her sexuality were revealed. She explained, "Like I said, you have a few negative situations and so then you just assume that's the way everyone is going to respond—even the people that love you, your family."

Kate's suicide attempt occurred in her senior year at the university. She said, "[the University] isn't *the* world, but at that point it was *my* world—it was all I knew." She explained her struggles to address the fraught intersection of her faith and sexuality during that period, saying,

> It was very frustrating because it wasn't going away and I was trying to do what I thought, like, find accountability, read God's word, pray— pray that God would take it away—and it wasn't happening so it was very frustrating. So then I was like, well maybe God *does* hate me . . . it wasn't really helping and so it almost kind of made it worse. Just because I started to hate that part of myself—I started to hate that and then I started to hate God and then I started to hate people around me. And then I was kind of like, well, there's really no point to live. And I was just like, if I die now, then I can just stop—because I came to a point where I realized that it was never going to go away.

And while Kate was raised to believe that suicide was a "really bad sin" and example of selfishness, she reasoned, "If I die now, I can get to leave and just be with God and I don't have to worry about being—not necessarily even just struggling with the sin—but I was like, if I live here, I'm going to be continually tempted."

Kate explained further the impact of the thinking behind her belief that God hated her, saying, "I felt like I was a disappointment to God." She continued,

> Even though I knew in my head, like, God doesn't make mistakes and he creates us in his image, I felt like he must have like, for me to have the worst of all the worst sins, I felt like he must be really angry at me or not love me as much. And I felt like even though I was trying to pursue him, I was trying to read God's word and I was trying to do the right things—what I thought was right—I just felt like I couldn't get into his good graces.

Her anger at God contributed to her sense of the unlivability of life due to the devastation of losing a relationship with God that she considered to be of central importance in her life. Kate said,

> I got really angry at [God]. And that was another reason, too, I think that I was suicidal. Because for most of my life I've known about God. I've been close to him since my teen years—that's when I accepted Christ. And when you have a bond with someone and all of the sudden it's like, it's different—it's, like, broken. I don't know, it's like life's not worth living, you know. Because you were in love with somebody and that relationship was broken.

While this period of her life were devastating for Kate, reflecting back about the period of her life leading up to her suicide attempt, Kate said,

> I would say it was very dark, rock bottom, very depressing, but also at the same time looking back now I feel like it was part of a necessary process in trying to figure out where I stood—trying to understand God. And it's definitely given me a lot more of an open mind to people that are struggling.

While she doesn't identify suicidal thoughts as a "good thing," she does say, looking back on this period of her life, "I really had to wrestle through a lot of who I was and what truth is and what morals are and a lot of the, I guess, deep questions of life that people try to figure out." And that struggle with important questions of identity and religious understanding she sees as helpful to her development as a person.

Her first positive experience sharing her sense of sexuality with another person occurred when she opened up to a friend over Skype. After Kate told her of her same-sex attraction, her friend wrote Kate a long letter with the basic message, "you're still the same person that I met three years ago and I don't look at you any differently and I love you." After having that positive experience telling one of Kate's closest friends, she felt better prepared to tell her parents and others.[2]

When Kate finally decided to talk with her family about her sexuality and struggles with suicidality, she was surprised by this openness to the conversation and the ensuing exploration of the intersection of Kate's sexuality and the family's faith tradition. She recounted,

> During that time, being open with [my parents] and then seeing that they were okay with it and that they were supportive and they wanted to help me. I guess that was kind of like, it just helped me because when you're in a dark situation where you're just like, you don't see any light and you're assuming because there's negativity from certain people . . . I guess like in that sea of negativity I saw, I guess I was afraid of being open with certain people. And then when I was, like, they wanted to help me, they wanted to be there with me, they wanted to help me figure out what I believe and wanted to support me. So that was very freeing, very uplifting, very encouraging.

Kate's mother responded in a way that was particularly heartening to Kate as she continues her journey to reconcile her faith and sexuality. She explained,

> We were talking about it and she was like, "I want to be open to what God has to say." And she basically said, "If being gay and being Christian is not wrong, I want to be okay with accepting that if that's what God's Word says." She's like, "Because I haven't researched it and there's things I haven't researched and I've just accepted them blindly because I've been taught them."

With Kate's own openness to exploration reflected in the response of her own mother, Kate began letting others in on the journey with her. After leaving the university where she felt under constant judgment, Kate met others who accepted her and the journey of exploration she was on. She summarizes the impact of these relationships, saying, "So I think meeting Christians that actually cared about me, that had a huge impact. And there weren't a lot, but here were some."

MIGUEL

Miguel is a thirty-year-old, Mexican/French, cisgender man who identifies as a "sexual being" in a same-sex relationship. He grew up in a nominally Catholic household and now identifies with "historical Christianity." His mother an father both came to the country undocumented from Mexico and gained citizenship in the United States.

In the fifth or sixth grade, Miguel recalls his first encounter with the concept of "religion," which he always thought of as part of this ethnicity. Upon asking his mother what religion they belonged to, she explained to Miguel that they were Catholic. His family attended church mostly on Christmas and Easter and other special occasions and, upon investigating further, he discovered his mother also practiced Santeria. Miguel mostly understood their family's sporadic church attendance as an opportunity to spend time with family and eat a big festive meal afterwards.

Reflecting back on his seven suicide attempts, Miguel says that sexuality played a part in them, but wasn't the catalyst. He explained that he "didn't have a pretty childhood." His family experienced periodic homelessness, living out of their car at one point, in a family homeless shelter at another, and several times in section eight apartments. He and his siblings were bullied for being the poorest kids in school and, on top of this targeting because of his family's economic status, he recalls the thought, "Oh, I'm different than everybody else in this sense: I'm not interested at all in girls." Adding one thing on top of the other, Miguel reflects back, "a little kid can only take so much." He explains his reasoning for the suicide attempts in hindsight,

So that's kind of how I had my self-reflection and why I think suicide seemed so logical, like, oh I'm in pain. Oh, I don't think it's ever going to stop. Oh, that seems like the solution for it. If I die then I no longer have any torment or pain. I don't have to get bullied anymore. And then I'm just kind of out of the equation. Also, being poor, I also thought . . . well then it'll be one less person they have to feed or take care of as well. So it was kind of all these things kind of combined.

Miguel's suicide experience stemmed from the comingling of all of these factors. As he said, "It was just having despair, hopelessness, I was being bullied at school, you know, not feeling understood or accepted."

But after a final failed attempt, Miguel ceased trying to kill himself. He said, "The fact that I attempted suicide seven times and that as you attempt suicide and you don't complete the suicide several times that just makes you more depressed because you can't even do that right." But he also reflected back on this decision to cease his suicide attempts with a theological reasoning as well:

I gave up on killing myself because I figured, obviously even if I want to kill myself, apparently God does not want me dead. And apparently your time is when your time is and apparently it's not my time. So that's kind of what kind of—I was at peace with, okay, I guess I should stop trying.

Miguel had a budding interest in religion when he was in his mid to late teenage years and went on the above-mentioned quest to decide upon a religious tradition to practice between the ages of fourteen and sixteen. After systematic exploration of a number of world religions, Miguel recalls being taken to church by a friend's family after spending the night at their house on a Saturday evening. While Miguel was in the youth room of the church with worship music planning, he recalls, "I had this tremendous, I had this emotion go over me and it was a sense of tremendous fear and tremendous warmth at the same time." He continues,

So then I thought, okay, I'll take this as a sign that, like, God, you're here whether you're here in the sense of presently here or here somewhere in the sense of like this religious place or church or whatever. I'm just going to take that as a sign because I didn't experience that anywhere else in any of the places that I went to. So then I said, well what better time to do the two-week thing and then, and my thought was, I'll do the two weeks and then this thing will be over and then I'll go on to whatever the next religion I can find. So I start doing the whole two-week thing. I talk to the youth pastor, I talk to the senior pastor, I tell them what I'm doing, I tell them what I need to do to fulfill whatever this religion is.

But instead of lasting two weeks, his exploration of protestant Christianity lasted for two years. He continued studying the tradition but didn't accept this as his own personal faith tradition until he was eighteen years old.

At eighteen, Miguel now belonged to a protestant Christian tradition and embraced this faith as his own. It was at that time when he began reading the verses in the biblical text about homosexuality. He says, "And then I had this idea, well if it's wrong, then what can I do about that? And so then I went to reparative therapy, or ex-gay ministry." He was twenty-one or twenty-two years old at the point he entered the ex-gay ministry, driving two-hours each way to access the group for biweekly meetings. "I bought a couple of books, I went to a little support group thing, journaled, did all that stuff," he said. "And it wasn't all bad. I learned things about, like, emotional dependency—which I realized I was like a poster child for, so I was able to work through that." But the group and its mission began to seem incredulous to Miguel. He reports going through a long period of seriously looking at the assumptions and teachings and methods of the group. He says, "I did that and then I realized that a lot of it was a bunch of crap."

Today, Miguel has reconciled his faith and sexuality, but holds a much more complex view of sexual identification than is often available in popular discourse. He says, "I'm just a sexual human being like everybody else. Because I don't really identify with gay, straight, or bi and I don't, I don't give that part of my identity a lot of hold in my life or a lot of power in labeling."

NOTES

1. Anna Lowenhaupt Tsing, *The Mushroom at the End of the World: On the Possibility of Life in Capitalist Ruins* (Princeton, NJ: Princeton University Press, 2015), 34.

2. Kate made an observation about the experience of many Christians in needing to "come out twice" to friends and loved ones. She said, "I don't know if this is typical of being in Christian circles, being gay and being Christian—but it's almost like you come out twice, sort of. I sort of feel like that. Just because the first time you're like, 'This is a sin, this is wrong, help me.' And people are supportive and then when you're like, 'Wait, I don't think this is unbiblical and this isn't something I can really change.' And then it's like you kind of have to resay it again and then—and that can be scary too, because you don't know. Because a lot of times Christians will support if you say it's a sin, but then if you're like, 'it isn't,' then it's like, you don't have that support."

THREE

Theological Ambush

Suicide is not monolithic. Our tendency to see all experiences of suicide as cut from the same cloth—typically as evidence of "mental illness" and assessed in psychological terms alone—reduces the complexity of this important lived experience. Psychiatrist R. D. Laing argues that if we look at a person's actions as "signs" of a "disease" we will impose these categories of thought on the person's behavior, making it unlikely that we will ever hear and understand what the person is attempting to communicate to us.[1] So while the conceptual tools of psychology may prove beneficial in suicide prevention and the treatment of mental illness related to suicide, this is ultimately a perspective limited in its ability to attend to the complexities of suicide experience. Thus, it should not become our *singular* vantage point.

By placing the dominant psychiatric and psychological understandings of suicide in critical abeyance, I aim to listen again for the messages suicide may hold through the process of hearing the voices of nine LGBTQ people who attempted suicide and survived. As Frank argues, "As stories tell people who they are, those people are embodied as much by stories as by their flesh. Stories, like bodies and in symbiosis with bodies, are people's dignity and their calamity."[2] Thus, stories and narratives that tell people who they are become of central importance in understanding the experience of LGBTQ suicide and religion.

Through these participant's stories, this chapter will explore how narratives "emplot" lives in ways that constrict possibilities for the livability of life. Chapters to come aim to expand the range of stories and narratives available for persons to draw upon, enlarging possibilities for the livability of life. The aim isn't "suicide prevention" in the traditional psychological sense of the term, dependent upon statistical analysis and empirical validation. As Bent Flyvbjerg argues, "From both an understanding-oriented and an action-oriented perspective, it is often more important to clarify the deeper causes behind a given problem than to describe the symptoms of the problem and how frequently they occur."[3] In a sense, the aim is still preventative, but in a more foundational sense: intervening in the narrative circumstances that set the stage for the precarity of life for some LGBTQ people leading to suicide attempt. So our aim is to ask what narratives—specifically *religious* and *theological* narratives—are implicated in suicide experience for LGBTQ people.

In the popular imagination, we tend to accept as fact that religion contributes to suicide ideation among LGBTQ people. In the social science literature, there is explicit focus on the "risk factor" that religion may become to LGBTQ people leading up to suicide attempt. In this chapter and the next I will look carefully for the ways in which particular stories, narratives, and emplotments are picked up and used as tools for understanding the self in relation to others and in relation to a presumed ultimate context. In the fifth and sixth chapters, I'll explore how some stories, narratives, and emplotments are refused and resisted and others picked up and used in life-preserving ways.[4]

This movement of analysis shifts between the inner and collective libraries, or between *individual* meaning-making and the attachment of an individual's stories to *widely circulating social narratives*. Many of these narratives confront us with what Parker describes as "an examination of how discourse functions ideologically, how it presents an oppressive version of the world that may feel suffocating to speakers and listeners, and which shows no way out."[5] So let us turn to the first-person narratives to look carefully at what is taking place at the *experiential level* in our common, but often unexamined, belief that religion contributes to suicidal ideation among LGBTQ people.

CONSTITUTIVE CONDEMNATION

In both the popular and professional imagination, there is little question that the condemnation of same-sex sexuality draws extensively upon the resources of the Christian theological tradition.[6] Beyond that popular assumption and basic social scientific finding, however, there has been little critical nuance in evaluating the complex intersection between LGBTQ suicide and religion. My theoretical assumption entering the research was that theologically laden narratives operate with an intensified force on the construction of a sense of self, as theological narratives propose to set life within a presumed ultimate context. But I didn't yet know the exact content of those narratives and how they operated to dispose us to listen to some of these stories more attentively and repeat them more frequently than others.[7] In other words, I am asking, *How do religious, theological, and spiritual narratives shape us at our deepest sense of who we are as human beings, speaking to the locus of our relationship with our own being?*

During our interview, Thomas summed up the messages he received about his emerging sense of sexuality early in his childhood with the statement, "You are an abomination. Your feelings are wrong before God." Thomas continued, rhetorically asking, "This part, your sexuality, which is below everything that you know—one of the foundations, the pillars of who you are, is wrong. And you're a child and you're trying to make sense of that. How can that not be violence?"

The description Thomas provides of his childhood encounters with theological narratives and emplotments related to his sexuality are illustrative of the "constitutive" potential for theological narratives that construct a sense of "soul" at a perceived level of coreness, connecting us to the locus of our own being in ways that enact a type of "soul violence." Thomas furthered this description, saying,

> Interesting thing about that, as a kid, if you're told you do something [and] it's an abomination, you can't tell the difference [between] being told what you do is an abomination and who you are is an abomination. I think it's impossible for a kid. And the primary message about that was so concerned with whether or not you had sinned that the fact that Jesus loved me no matter what, now and forever, was lost. So I stayed alone for more than a decade.

It is important to note one theme early on that will arise again and again in participants' stories: *competing theological narratives*. In the competing theological narratives of Jesus' love and the condemnation of same-sex sexuality, Thomas's narrative habitus was very early on shaped by narratives of "abomination" that introduced an ontological position of spiritual abjection, sedimented over time through repeated contact with this theological narrative, and set on the plane of ultimacy through theological justification (e.g., *God* sees you this way).

Beyond what is *spoken*, Judith Butler illuminates the interpellative potential of *silence*—that is, the ability of *silence*, as well as speech, to bring into being a sense of identity for us. She argues, "Indeed, one can be interpellated, put in place, given a place, through silence, through not being addressed, and this becomes painfully clear when we find ourselves preferring the occasion of being derogated to the one of not being addressed at all."[8] Thomas described the power of silence in his own childhood experience of constitutive condemnation, saying,

> You're straight until proven guilty. And the messages that I got, not only from the ministers—just about any minister . . . [they] didn't have to quote like Leviticus and Deuteronomy. All they had to do was, like, imply it. All they had to do was not talk about being gay as if it was real. All they had to do was only talk about heterosexual families. All they had to do was only address men and women relationships.

And beyond conspicuous silence, Thomas continued by explaining that once the message of condemnation was in place as a part of one's inner library, all that was necessary to re-activate the power of that dormant narrative was a particular intonation or vocal inflection to signal the condemnatory message. He says,

> It's tone—the tone of what you say. And it's like a bell that goes off. The first time you hear a bell you know what a bell sounds like. The first time you hear that you're an abomination, you remember that tone. And they don't have to say it ever again in those words. All they have to do is say something that indicates that you don't fit into their understanding and their understanding is more important than you are. You know you've just heard again, "You're an abomination."

The key theoretical feature of the perspective I am developing here is the particular role of *theological* narratives, which builds upon but differs from the work of Butler and others on the constitutive and interpellative potential of narrative. If narrative has the constitutive potential to construct our "inner" sense of self, shaping our narrative habitus, and the interpellative power to "position" us in varied ways in relation to social others, it's important to note that *theological* narratives purport to say something "true" about the core of our beings and position us on an *ultimate scale*. We may, then, see LGBTQ suicide related to a subjective form of violence operating on a theological plane of existence—hailing one into a subject position set within a presumed ultimate context. Here, too, Thomas illuminates the process of theological interpellation that is constitutively condemnatory, saying,

> I very gradually got the impression that most of what was inside me should be kept separate from everybody, from the world—my attraction to men, my confusion about women . . . The most horrible violence is that the message that comes through the word itself is a message of hope and the feeling that you get from the people who are saying the words is a message of violence. And you're a child. A message of damnation—be clear. The words say a message of hope and the person says a message of damnation or condemnation. And you're a child! You're trying to make sense of that.

Here again, we glimpse the competing theological narratives doing their work on Thomas. Drawing upon the Bible, Thomas's childhood self-understanding was shaped both by biblical messages of love and biblically fueled messages of "damnation" concerning what was "inside" him, interpellating, *hailing* him, into the position of an abomination in relation to his religious tradition and the social others practicing that tradition alongside him. His commentary on his childhood resonates with Didier Eribon's argument that discourses of *insult* define one's horizon of relation to the world, producing "a fateful feeling in a child or an adolescent who feels himself or herself to be contravening the world's order as well as a lasting and even permanent feeling of insecurity, anxiety, and even terror and panic."[9]

Here Thomas brings out a theme in the research interviews that took me by surprise. While I fully expected the themes of condemnatory speech, rejection, and theologically denigrating discourses to feature prominently in my interviews with participants, I began to note a specific distress brought about by the way theological language comes into conflict with itself (e.g., Thomas says, "The words say a message of hope and the person says a message of damnation."). I soon realized that this "theological doublespeak" gives significant shape to the way theological condemnation takes place in LGBTQ lives, speaking to the coreness of their relationship with their own being, or soul.

THEOLOGICAL DOUBLESPEAK

While the social scientific literature on LGBTQ suicide speaks to the role of religious condemnatory messages in the psychological and emotional well-being of LGBTQ people, most of the literature fails to take into account the complex ways theological narratives operate to set life within an ultimate context. This is a key feature of this book's perspective on the role of religious and theological narratives in LGBTQ suicide experience. Theological narratives surround many LGBTQ people throughout childhood and adolescence, moving narratives from the library of collectively held religious material into the inner library and cultivating the narrative habitus inhabited by the LGBTQ individual—that "collection of stories in which life is formed and that continue to shape lives."[10]

Many of the theological narratives explored by the research participants in this study provided *meaningful* and *life-sustaining* narrative material, shaping the individual's relationship to family and friends, providing vocational direction, and giving one a sense of larger meaning by setting life within a presumed ultimate context. One of the clearest examples of the co-occurrence of theologically damaging and theologically life-sustaining narratives is exemplified in the ways several participants made vocational decisions.

For example, Tandiwae spent the bulk of her young adult years in music ministry, planning to follow this vocational trajectory for the remainder of her career until she was kicked out of her positions of service within two churches after coming out as lesbian. Thomas described an ongoing sense of desire for service to the church and continues to consider going to seminary. Florence, too, served throughout her life in a variety of ecclesial and Christian educational contexts in the performance of sacred music and leadership in worship, and she continues to work in a religiously affiliated institution as an out lesbian religious leader. Some element of Christian service as central to one's self-understanding or vocational trajectory was present at some point in the lives of a majority of my research participants.

Recognizing the important constitutive role that theological narratives hold for many LGBTQ people, the damage inflicted by mixed theological messages began making more sense. Condemnatory, denigrating theological messages hold so much power to damage because other, more positive and sustaining theological narratives are so constitutively central to many LGBTQ people's sense of being and purpose. When sustaining theological messages inculcated in participants' childhood begin coming into conflict with the condemnatory theological messages experienced in relation to their sexual orientation or gender identity, they became difficult narrative strands to separate, as they emerged form the same theological sources (e.g., the Bible) and often from the same persons and communities (e.g., family, pastor, church members).

Another participant, Louise, describes this theological doublespeak in broad terms related to her sense of internal "chaos" in her adolescent life. She says,

> It was very stressful. And I think because so many of those things contradict themselves too, because you hear, you know, "Oh its black, not white," from one person and you hear, "Oh it's white, not black," from another person in regards to either gender or religion or morals or whatever. It was just confusing. Especially, again, like the first time it was just total chaos. Like, none of this makes sense. Nothing makes sense. Everything is chaos.

Kate, another participant who grew up the child of a minister, first on the mission field abroad and later in a congregational setting in the United States, began experiencing theological doublespeak when she attended a fundamentalist Protestant Christian university where she heard frequent condemnatory messages about same-sex sexuality. Kate describes how denigrating messages came into conflict with what she learned about God's love under her father's preaching and religious guidance:

> I felt like I was a disappointment to God. Even though I knew in my head, like, God doesn't make mistakes and he creates us in his image. I felt like he must have, like, for me to have the worst of all the worst sins, I felt like he must be really angry at me or not love me as much. And I felt like even though I was trying to pursue him, I was trying to read God's word and I was trying to do the right things—what I thought was right—I just felt like I couldn't get into his good graces. I felt like I wasn't, even though he says, "You're my child and you're pure in my sight and I've covered you in the blood," I don't know, I guess in my mindset I was thinking God hates me, I don't understand why he's allowed me to do this. Because I feel like there's a reason for everything. And since I wasn't, since it just seemed normal and natural

to me, I was like, well maybe he created me like this. I don't know why he would do that, it seems really cruel.

Similarly, Louise described these conflicting messages experienced during her childhood attendance at Catholic Mass, saying,

> It was also very confusing because half of Mass, "Accept your neighbor, love your neighbor, do good, do good in the world, live like Christ, be Christ-like, and whatnot." And then the other half of it would be, "You're going to hell if you do this. You're going to hell if you do that. Don't love this person, you can only love this person. And these are the criterion for who you should accept in your life," basically was what I was hearing. And I was like, wait a second, I don't, I'm not, I don't fit that criteria.

This is illustrative of the constitutive power of *ambient theological messages*, which do not have to be delivered directly to an LGBTQ person in order for "uptake" into the inner library to occur. Indeed, Louise was not and still is not "out" to her family about her sexual and gender identities as a pansexual, gender queer/pangender/fluid person. These ambient messages, nevertheless, became constitutive of her narrative habitus, as they do for many LGBTQ people, offering up the stories that form and shape life. This often leaves one to work through the meaning of these vastly divergent theological messages in isolation, as most research participants did in their childhood and adolescent years.

Thomas illustrates the way that the narratives that populate the inner library come into conflict with larger discourses within collective libraries when speaking about his own suicide attempt in ways that were, in his words, "impossible to reconcile." He goes on to explain:

> The message of Christ is love and the message of Christ is damnation. In my heart it's love, and in the world it's damnation. And they use the same words. It was maddening. And a mind can't do that. A mind cannot fix that. Ever. It's impossible. It's insane . . . And when you're paralyzed between those two things—God hates me and God loves me—when you're beaten enough with that and you reach the point where, like, "I'm done." It's a pain. It's a terrible pain. Maybe stronger people than me can deal with that pain longer. I couldn't. And eventually, you know, I don't think people kill themselves because they want to die. I think they kill themselves because the pain is too bad . . . There was no way to figure it out and it was so early in my life that it was established—like as a boy. You know? It was so early that all my life I'm just like, "Oh my God, this is awful! What an awful place to be! God loves you and hates you. What the fuck is that?" . . . The feelings of that, "God loves me, God hates me. All this stuff in my life is bad, and all this stuff is good. Oh my God." You don't think that, you just feel it.

I followed up, asking if Thomas meant that the phrase, "you just feel it," meant felt in his body and he confirmed that it was, indeed, a bodily sense.

Elaine Graham argues for the importance of placing the *body* at the center of theological construction, as the body is the surface upon which the most controversial and pressing dilemmas in theology are made flesh.[11] The theological dilemma of LGBTQ bodies is a primary example, and the theological doublespeak experienced by LGBTQ persons seems to, indeed, become flesh in corporeal feelings of pain and chaos and unresolvable tension. The importance of focusing on the embodied experience that Thomas points us to is further elucidated by Didier Eribon who writes about the effects of shame, hatred, and violence in relation to the formation of "self" for gay persons. He states,

> The long-term effects of insult and hatred . . . write themselves into the body; they act by way of your own submission to the injunction they carry, your own consent to the order they enforce—that your personality and your desires must remain hidden, that the line must be toed. They command you to act "as if." They necessitate a permanent effort to ensure that none of your emotions, feelings, or desires are ever revealed.[12]

In this vein, Graham draws upon the work of Bourdieu to argue, "Such a *habitus* is also, I contend, necessarily embodied. Social structures are inscribed on bodily activity."[13] As Eribon makes clear, part of the embodied experience that we must take into account are the emotions, feelings, and desires of research participants—all part of the narrative habitus—shaped by socio-theological discourses communicating insult and hatred that "write themselves onto the body" of queer people. In Thomas's experience, the emotion and the physical, bodily experience of "pain" resulted from the constant competition of theological narratives ("God loves me, God hates me") shaping the habitus and constructing a sense of his relation to his own being, or soul.

Gay Catholic theologian and priest James Alison describes this theological "double-bind" in words remarkably similar to Thomas above. Alison autobiographically notes,

> My own story has been one in which I knew at some level, since the wrenching experience of falling in love with a school colleague when I was nine years old, that the word of God was one of love. But as I grew I was unable to allow myself to hear it in the depths of my being. Those depths were utterly prisoner to the voices of hatred which form us as gay people . . . canonised by an ecclesiastical voice which has been so tied up in all this that it has been incapable of discerning between the voice of the world and the voice of God. So it says: love, and do not love; be, and do not be. The voice of God has been presented as a double bind, which is actually far more dangerous than a simple mes-

sage of hate, since it destabilises being into annihilation, and thinks that annihilation to be a good thing.[14]

Alison goes on to say, "The true horror is not that there is a 'they' out there, doing this to a pure and innocent 'us,' but that we are all deeply personally involved in the 'they,' finding it both necessary and apparently righteous to hold on to vanities and apostasise from the source of lovingkindness."[15]

The convergence and conflict of theological narratives from the inner library and those from the collective library were evident when Thomas said, "Inside me, I would know that God loves me and outside me I would know that God hates me." He continued,

> But as a child coming up, if you can't reconcile that, if everything in you says God is good and everything, and the only thing you have to get your needs met says that you are an abomination and God hates you, the result is insanity. It's inevitable. So like all I could do as a person was pray to this God that I just believed in. I couldn't figure it out—he loves me, he hates me. Whatever! Please help! And he did! But I've never been able to talk about it. And that's what I ended up praying for. That's where I put my feet. I can't answer any of the arguments. I know that God loves us. And it's not based on any of the arguments, cause I can't figure that shit out. It's too much for me.

These converging and conflicting theological narratives that exist side-by-side on the shelves of LGBTQ people's inner libraries are the source of great conflict that often requires an LGBTQ person to work through the pain and distress of this conflict in solitude. And besides the pain of isolation amid such emotionally draining theological work, the results of such doublespeak gave shape to a sense of soul for these research participants in painful and debilitating ways. Theological doublespeak produced an embodied sense of internal chaos for Louise, embodied pain for Thomas, and sense of Divine cruelty for Kate.

It is well noted in the social science literature that family, peer, and other social rejection are major factors in the social science literature on LGBTQ suicide. We must, however, remember Charles Taylor's admonition when approaching the social scientific literature when he says that that, most often, however tightly the dependence of the individual upon the social is conceived, "it is seen in causal terms, and not as touching our very identity."[16] It is important for scholars and professionals concerned by the phenomenon of LGBTQ suicide to begin thinking beyond *causal* terms and toward *constitutive* ones. The research material herein helps to move us in this direction by pointing to the ways that theological messages are not just causative of familial, peer, or other social rejection, but the theological nature of the discourse—setting life within a presumed ultimate context, speaking to the locus of our relationship to our own being—produces an *intensification effect*, providing interprellative force to interpersonal rejection.

WEIGHING REJECTION "HERE" AND "HEREAFTER"

Many of the theological messages of condemnation represented in the interview material above are ambient messages taking place in the social and religious milieu that an individual inhabits (and that constitutively inhabit the individual). These stand in distinction to many messages that are *overtly* directed at the LGBTQ individual specifically (though these direct messages are quite common, too). Thus, for an experience-near perspective on the ways that religious and theological narratives intersect with LGBTQ suicide experience, it is important to look at the theological-ly laden constitutive forms of condemnation as connected to, but not synonymous with, the more direct interpersonal experiences of rejection. This will help us to understand the ways that theological discourse itself, not just its direct communication to an LGBTQ individual in messages of rejection, becomes constitutive of a sense of coreness, or soul. Though direct, personal rejection and familial or ecclesial expulsion are suppor-tive of the constitutive theological narratives of condemnation, the two experiences seem to occur independently and, at times, interdependently. One participant for whom both of these strands of rejection occurred quite clearly is Silas.

Silas exemplifies the themes that emerged in several interviews of rejection between the "here" of her family and her university and the "hereafter" of her fundamentalist Christian religious teachings about the fate of persons who engage in same-sex relationships. In her narrative and several others, the theological narratives of rejection serve to inten-sify the familial rejection or ecclesial expulsion in ways that become a *constitutive* experience of condemnation.

Nowhere is this intensification effect clearer in the research interviews than when participants talked about the extent to which their constitutive sense of condemnation extended beyond the social sphere to a sphere of ultimacy, often symbolized by condemnation in the "hereafter." This im-brication of the "here" and "hereafter" of condemnation informed suicide attempts for a number of participants in surprising ways. For example, Silas reported:

> And then we have eternity . . . I thought, you know, here I was con-demned and rejected and so that meant not only here, that meant eter-nally. So things didn't matter as much. Because we were taught in the Christian realm that you're always living for the rewards of the after-life, and if you feel like you're already condemned and doomed, it's like, what does it matter? . . . Yeah, condemned Christian in this life and the afterlife. Which didn't leave a whole lot of room for care.

Though I did not ask specific questions about beliefs in the afterlife and how suicide attempts were influenced by these beliefs, these themes emerged in a number of other interviews as well. While I was unsurprised to hear that theological themes of condemnation in the afterlife were a part of the collective library of theological narratives informing the religious perspective of participants leading up to their suicide attempts, I *was* surprised by how these narratives were weighted in relation to social rejection for many participants. The intensification effect seemed to work in both directions—from the theological intensifying the social, to the social intensifying the theological.

For example, Miguel, who grew up Catholic, stated that his belief about suicide at the time of his multiple attempts was that it was an "ultimate sin" from which there was no time to repent and, thus, automatically resulted in one's soul going to hell. Then, to my surprise, he said, "But I had thought, well at least I'll be dead and if I'm going to be in hell in eternity, I feel like I'm already in hell . . . So, you know, it didn't matter to me." Louise, who also grew up Catholic, similarly reported, "I wasn't so much worried about Heaven and Hell as I was, like, life on earth . . . as a kid, I was never like, 'Oh my God, I'm going to go to hell!' It was like, life is going to be hell on earth if I'm not able to connect with my peers and my family." Finally, Thomas relates his own childhood experience of theological condemnation to his sense of dependence on others, saying,

> The message of Christ is hope, love, unconditional. Done. Anything that implies anything different—the feeling of it, an understanding that messes with it—anything at all, just get your shit straight. That's wrong. But as a child you cannot do that. You need the world. You have to have the world. You can't exist alone . . . A child needs the world, somehow. Maybe I think God designed it that way. Maybe [it] helps knit the world together.

Surprisingly to me, social rejection and interpersonal strife seemed far weightier than beliefs about condemnation in the afterlife to the few interview participants who broached the subject.[17]

My own assumption going into the interview research was that the constitutive effectives of the theological narratives upon the sense of soul were far weightier, intensifying the social elements of familial and social rejection, but not necessarily the other way around. The interviews, however, convinced me of the ways that, at times, the *social experience* intensifies the *theological narrative's* constitutive power as well. As the book progresses into the next chapter, the analysis remains attentive to the ways that this complexity shows up in the narratives that are indicative of "subjective precarity" in the suicide experience of participants.

THEOLOGICAL NARRATIVES AND
THE AMBUSH OF QUEER SOULS

Before moving into the next chapter, however, it is helpful to explore with a bit more theoretical depth what exactly is taking place at this experience-near, granular level between the suicide experience of LGBTQ people and the religious and theological narratives that populate their collective and inner libraries.

First, it is important to understand the function of "constitution" and "interpellation" as I've used the terms here and will continue to do so throughout the book. Judith Butler inquires into the constitutive and interpolative potential of language, asking, "Could language injure us if we were not, in some sense, linguistic beings, beings who require language in order to be? Is our vulnerability to language a consequence of our being constituted within its terms?"[18] In reply, Butler contends that language is the "condition of possibility" for a subject, rather than merely a means of expression.[19] As a "condition of possibility," our self-perceived ontological status—our sense of our own beingness in the world—is dependent largely upon the constitutive effects of language. Narratives moving from the collective to the individual libraries condition our possibility as speaking and spoken subjects, providing the constitutive building blocks from which our sense of relation to our own being, *our souls*, are patched together. Or, as Eribon contends, "individual" subjectivity is always collective, as individuals are always socialized within groups.[20] I hope that, by now, these constitutive and interpolative functions of language are evidenced in the narratives from participants above, and they will continue to be foregrounded in the participant narratives that follow.

Psychologist Jerome Bruner explains that the constitutive potential of the symbolic meaning of language is dependent upon the "human capacity to internalize such a language and to use its *system* of signs as an interpretant in this 'standing for' relationship."[21] It is the ability of the linguistic symbol to represent the ontological beingness of another human that holds the potential to enact violence on the level at which our sense of self, or our *soul*, is constituted through language and narratives. Our ontological status, however tentative, is dependent upon the constitutive effects of language. That is why, as Butler argues, we may even cling to the names and terms that cause us pain, as they at very least offer us a form of social and discursive existence.[22]

Finally, it is vital to see the function of interpellation operating within theological language to *introduce* a reality, rather than to simply report on an already existing reality. This is the "inaugurative" potential of interpellation, establishing one's subjectivity by sedimenting the reality being introduced over the course of time.[23] This became especially clear in the narrative of Thomas above related to the narrative of "abomination." The interpellative ability of language bespeaks the ability of narrative to bring one into *social* beingness. Butler points to the importance of interpellations that "hail" a subject into being for understanding the process of "subject-formation" and the "embodied, participatory *habitus*," constituting us discursively and interpellating us socially.[24]

These conceptual tools accord with the pragmatist theological thrust of this research, attentive to what Davaney describes as an insistence that we evaluate our theologies with the "fullest cognizance possible of their consequences," always attempting to mitigate the unjust and tragic outcomes made possible by theology's constitutive and interpellative potential.[25] This theoretical vantage point guides the development of my analysis to take shape around the above three illustrative subthemes in relation to theological constitution and interpellation: constitutive condemnation, theological doublespeak, and weighing rejection "here" and "hereafter."

Importantly, Frank notes, "Sometimes, stories that have no place in people's inner library still teach those people who they can be; stories have a capacity for *narrative ambush*."[26] Freighted with theological weight—purporting to set life within an ultimate context, speaking about the presumed "true nature" of one's relation to one's own being—religious narratives have a particularly potent potential to ambush queer souls. These narratives that may have no place in queer people's inner library, nevertheless, do their constitutive work on our souls, hailing us into being in ways that make life, at times, precarious. The theological ambush of queer souls, iterated in the stories above, leads us into an experience-near exploration of the *outcomes* of this narratival work on queer folk. Now that we have explored some of the ways that religious, theological, and spiritual narratives shape LGBTQ people at our deepest sense of who we are as human beings, speaking to the locus of our relationship with our own being, we turn to the experiences of "subjective precarity" *induced* by the constitutive work of these narratives upon our queer souls.

NOTES

1. R.D. Laing, *The Divided Self: An Existential Study in Sanity and Madness* (Harmondsworth, UK: Penguin, 1960), 33.

2. Arthur W. Frank, *Letting Stories Breathe: A Socio-Narratology* (Chicago: University of Chicago, 2010), 146.

3. Bent Flyvbjerg, "Five Misunderstandings about Case-Study Research," in *Qualitative Research Practice*, ed. Clive Seale, Giampetro Gobo, Jaber F. Gubrium, and David Silverman (London: Sage, 2007), 395.

4. Frank, *Letting Stories Breathe*, 51.

5. Ian Parker, *Qualitative Psychology: Introducing Radical Research* (New York: Open University Press, 2005), 90.

6. Kathleen Erwin, "Interpreting the Evidence: Competing Paradigms and the Emergence of Lesbian and Gay Suicide as a 'Social Fact,'" *International Journal of Health Services* 23, no. 3 (1993): 439.

7. Frank, *Letting Stories Breathe*, 53.

8. Judith Butler, *Excitable Speech: A Politics of the Performative* (New York: Routledge, 1997), 27.

9. Didier Eribon, *Insult and the Making of the Gay Self*, trans. Michael Lucey (Durham, NC: Duke University Press, 2004), 65.

10. Frank, *Letting Stories Breathe*, 49.

11. Elaine Graham, *Words Made Flesh: Writings in Pastoral and Practical Theology* (London: SCM Press, 2009), 116. Graham's essay in this text titled, "'Only Bodies Suffer': Embodiment, Representation and the Practice of Ethics," is influential in the shaping of my thought about the methodological placement of embodiment in the research frame.

12. Eribon, *Insult and the Making of the Gay Self*, 98–99.

13. Graham, *Words Made Flesh*, 158.

14. James Alison, *Faith Beyond Resentment: Fragments Catholic and Gay* (New York: Crossroad, 2001), 94.

15. Alison, *Faith Beyond Resentment*, 94.

16. Charles Taylor, *Human Agency and Language: Philosophical Papers 1* (New York: Cambridge University Press, 1985), 8.

17. Not every participant who described thoughts about the afterlife believed they were condemned to hell. Kate, for example, seemed to believe that since she had not yet engaged in same-sex sexual activity, killing herself would take her out of the realm of temptation. She stated, "It was just like, if I die now, I can get to leave and just be with God and I don't have to worry about being—not necessarily even just struggling with the sin—but I was like, if I live here, I'm going to be continually tempted. That was my mindset. There was more potential for me to fall into sin—what I thought was sin. So I was like, if I just die now then I don't have to, you know, I can just spend time with God. But the longer I'm here on earth, it's like, I think I'm always going to battle with this and it's always going to affect my relationship with God. So I just thought, you know, it'd be better to just go."

18. Butler, *Excitable Speech*, 1–2.

19. Butler, *Excitable Speech*, 28.

20. Eribon, *Insult and the Making of the Gay Self*, xvii.

21. Jerome Bruner, *Acts of Meaning* (Cambridge, MA: Harvard University Press, 1990), 69.

22. Butler, *Excitable Speech*, 26.

23. Butler, *Excitable Speech*, 33–34.

24. Butler, *Excitable Speech*, 153.

25. Sheila Greeve Davaney, *Pragmatic Historicism: A Theology for the Twenty-First Century* (Albany, NY: State University of New York Press, 2000), 165.

26. Frank, *Letting Stories Breathe*, 58. Emphasis in original.

FOUR

Soul Violence

A central question of many religious traditions is that of how we are positioned in relation to God. Are we partners in relation to God who is at work in the world? Are we separated from God and in need of reunion? Do we have any potential for proximity to the deity at all?

This is an important question in the lives of LGBTQ people too. Churches have long purported to know something about how LGBTQ people are positioned in relation to God—often in an oppositional position—and how that relationship needs changing. This question arises in the narratives of several participants in this research. As a researcher, I am interested more specifically in how certain religious, spiritual, and theological narratives purport to position human beings in relation to God—or at least the word/symbol "God"—forming the "deep myths" that constitute a person's sense of self, or soul. Specifically, what does the narrative placement of human lives within a presumed "ultimate context" through theological narratives do to shape the livability of life for LGBTQ people, opening and closing possibilities for both flourishing and precarity?

In this chapter I ask how narratives regarding LGBTQ identifications come to operate theologically—setting one's life in the world within a presumed ultimate context—contributing to the precarity of one's subjectivity leading to a suicide attempt. First, this exploration requires some comment about how I theoretically arrived upon the notion of "subjective precarity" before looking more specifically at how I believe this narrative production of precarity affects the lives of some of LGBTQ people leading to a suicide attempt.

SUBJECTIVE PRECARITY

Arthur Frank, a primary influence in developing the methods for this research, argues that this type of inquiry "sets aside, at least provisionally, the idea of people telling stories, and it thinks instead of stories imposing themselves on people, and these people then being limited to representing their lives according to whatever imagination the stories make available."[1] The process of stories imposing themselves on people—that is, stories in the collective library attaining import into inner libraries—is key to my narrative understanding of identify formation. The stories we tell about ourselves over time are constitutive of our sense of who we are as human beings. But perhaps more powerfully, the stories that are told *about* us, "imposing themselves" on us make some narratives we might hold about ourselves more tellable and others less so. Some stories ambush us, forcibly inserting themselves in our inner library.

Hilde Lindemann Nelson describes identity as "constituted from the first-person perspective through the loosely connected stories we weave around the things about us that matter most to us: the acts, experiences, and characteristics we care most about, and the roles, relationships, and values to which we are most deeply committed."[2] While this may seem, at first glance, a very individualistic process, Nelson reminds us that other people's stories about an individual are often more authoritative than the person's own self-told stories. Our sense of "identity" is always contingent on others, making identity formation a social process. As Nelson says, "Who I am depends to some extent on who other people will let me be."[3]

In this vein, psychiatrist R. D. Laing's concept of "ontological insecurity" becomes helpful in assessing the narratives that follow. Laing describes this state consisting of a sense that one's identity and autonomy are always in question, that one's personal sense of consistency or cohesiveness is lacking, and a feeling that one is "more insubstantial than substantial, and unable to assume that the stuff [one] is made if is genuine, good, valuable."[4] Commenting on Laing's study, Burkitt adds that in a state of ontological insecurity, the body "comes to feel dead, like a hollow shell: a lifeless object in the world among other lifeless objects."[5]

As a lens for viewing LGBTQ suicide experience, Laing's concept can be developed further toward a concept of "subjective precarity," influenced by the work of Foucault, Butler, and others. Judith Butler describes the fundamental sense of life's precarity in the ways we are always "given over to the other" from life's natality. She argues that this means that "we are vulnerable to those we are too young to know and to judge and, hence, vulnerable to violence; but also vulnerable to another range of touch, a range that includes the eradication of our being at one end, and the physical support for our lives at the other."[6]

When the vulnerability of this fundamental precarity leads toward the damage, or even *eradication*, of our being, Eribon notes that this painful and profound experience eventuates in a break "within one's own individual subjectivity."[7] Nelson notes that this destabilizing, precarity-producing process occurs when the dominant narratives and discourses diminishes the respectability and worth of an Other, preventing someone from occupying valuable social roles or entering certain meaningful and desirable relationships that are, as illustrated above, constitutive of one's identity. She notes that this identity damage is exacerbated when one "endorses, as part of her self-concept, a dominant group's dismissive or exploitative understanding of her group, and loses or fails to acquire a sense of herself as a worthy of full moral respect."[8]

Through engaging the interview material, I will develop proposals for understanding how the effects of a sense of "subjective precarity" sets life on edge, bringing about a sense of precarity in the livability of life. Specifically, I will attend to the *experience* of precarity, rather than its conditions of development, by exploring the affective themes of feeling internally unmoored, feeling hidden, and feeling trapped. In keeping with my methodological focus, I give particular attention to the ways religious, spiritual, and theological narratives related to these experiences of precarity.

FEELING INTERNALLY UNMOORED

Florence shared rich detail about a dimension of her experience in college when she began to embrace her sense of attraction to other women while, at the same time, acquiescing to giving up her Christian religious commitments, as she thought that these two were fundamentally mutually exclusive. As she began this process of giving up her Christian identifications—albeit temporarily, as it turned out—in order to embrace her attraction to other women, Florence made a romantic invitation to a woman who had become one of her best friends. But when her friend responded with rejection and mild disgust at the notion of a lesbian relationship, Florence described being unable to see any future for her life. She describes this period of her college life, stating, "It really felt like I lost everything. I lost all of my anchors in life. And I couldn't see a way forward . . . it just felt like everything was done. I couldn't see a future."

After this episode of rejection, Florence went back to her dorm room and attempted to kill herself. In further exploring how this sense of anchorlessness affected her sense of self and the connections this experience may have to the term "soul," Florence described the way that her sense of coreness was affected:

> I think when I'm talking about the core, that sort of inner sense—I think that's probably what I would call a soul. And that sense that, you know, as I was trying to own a lesbian identity, the sense that my soul

was just sort of rotting was definitely leading up to that—I would probably use the term spirit—but like that sense that the thing that was my center, my heart, my, you know, connection to the divine was just rotting away.

Here, Florence's comments upon her sense of her "core," her "inner sense," her "center" gradually "rotting away," paired with her comment above that without the anchors in her life she had once depended upon she could no longer see a future for her life, harkens back to Burkitt's commentary on R. D. Laing's notion of "ontological insecurity" as a feeling of the body being dead, "like a hollow shell: a lifeless object in the world."[9] In narratival terms, this experience points to what Mark Freeman terms "narrative foreclosure," when the narrative of one's life seems to have a stopping point beyond which there is no more story to be lived. Florence describes this foreclosure in evocative terms, saying, "I don't think I really understood why . . . it felt so like my life was over. I didn't really know what all the components were of that in the moment of it. I just knew that I felt like everything had fallen apart and there was no future."

According to Freeman, narrative foreclosure is characterized by the conviction that one's story—the constitutive material of life's livability—is effectively over.[10] Nelson's work adds depth to this developing understanding of narrative foreclosure in Florence's narrative by illuminating the ways that narratives impinge upon a person's ability to act on a particular identity. Nelson says, "No matter how fundamental her commitment to the value around which that identity centers, and no matter how centrally the story of that commitment figures into her self-constituting autobiography, the identity is not hers. She cannot claim an identity that has no outlet for its expression."[11] This is an especially helpful way to view the conflict point in Florence's story, as the religious discourses surrounding her suggested that the fundamental commitments she held toward Christian faith practice could not be maintained in relation to her developing sense of lesbian identity, and the person to whom Florence first disclosed her lesbian identity refused to recognize "Christian lesbian" as a morally valid identity.

Similar themes of a loss of moorings arose in other interviews related to participants' suicide attempt. In a lengthy exchange with Louise, I asked her, if her life were a book, what the chapter containing her suicide attempt would be titled. To this question, she responded:

Louise: Immediately I thought, The Flood. That was like my very first, because, like, when you're dealing with, or when I was dealing with depression and anxiety to an extreme, it kind of felt like I was being flooded—like I was drowning. It was so overwhelming. And then it was sort of like, it kind of reminded me of, like I don't know, religious—kind of like the Noah thing, like, that reminded me of that. I guess that would be the title of the chapter during which I attempted my first suicide. Again, it's probably because it's just super, it's like when you can't breathe—that's exactly what it's like.

Cody: So what was it like for you to have that sense of overwhelm, not being able to breathe? How did that come about for you in your life?

Louise: I wouldn't say it was sudden. It wasn't like, you know, I just had, like it was one really bad year. It was kind of like a buildup over time . . . It was dealing with not feeling accepted like personality wise, which had nothing to do with my sexuality or gender. But I think that was kind of an extension of what I identified as, which was also really confusing. That's the other thing, like, especially when I was that young, it was just, it wasn't, "this is what's bothering me," it was just chaos. It was like, I couldn't articulate any of it, even in my own head because I didn't really understand or was able to grasp exactly what was going on. So it was like, um, yeah it was just chaos. It wasn't like, now if I'm having anxiety or depression or anything like having suicidal thoughts, I know where the sources, because I kind of like have a better grasp on what's going on. But as far as like gender and identity and personality and things like that, it was just, it was completely overwhelming. It was nonsense.

Over time, Louise described the way that a sense of overwhelm and chaos—experiences related to the developing theme of subjective precarity—led her to experience the unlivability of life, rather than a very specific will to die. She says,

> It was just, like, and it wasn't even, "I want to die," it was just, "I don't want to live." And that's both times. It was never like, it was never like, "I want to die." It was just, "I'm done living. I'm just exhausted." Like, I'll never fit in. I don't fit in. I'm never going to be accepted. This world is mean and cruel and hard and why bother, basically.

For Florence, nearly two decades removed from her suicide attempt during college, the power of these feelings of internal unmooring—trouble with the "core" of being—continue to arise in unexpected ways:

> Yeah, I think the other thing that has always—it always sort of surprises me how that feeling can recur. The feeling of just questioning what that core is and that continues to be a struggle even now—fifteen or twenty years later. There are those moments when I think, what if? What if this is not the right narrative that I'm telling myself? Or, what if there really is something that is still sort of rotten at the core in how I live my life and who I am in the world? And those moments still take me by surprise . . . there'll still be the times when someone says some really homophobic thing and all of the sudden I'm back in that place again. Or there's that spark of feeling that comes back. And I think that

always—I think it just takes me aback that it doesn't necessarily go away. And trying to figure out what it means to continue to feel like you have to negotiate that.

Florence's statement is illustrative of the lasting effects of the sedimentation of the narratives that constitute one's sense of self, such that the power of these discourses to set life on edge continue to be activated many years after the initial contact between these narratives in the collective library with one's inner library sources. For many, the interpellative power of these narratives to bring one into social being in relation to one's community led to many years of negotiating these feelings of internal unmooring both in isolation and, at times, with the help of others when it was judged that others may be more helpful than harmful.

FEELING HIDDEN

A second prominent theme throughout many of the participants' narratives was the feeling of being hidden within. When popular discourse on LGBTQ lives is saturated with talk of being "in" or "out of the closet," it was surprising that very few of the participants spoke of their experience with the clear binary language that the dichotomy ("in" versus "out") that the discourse of "the closet" provides. Instead participants spoke of their experience with a greater degree of complexity, noting the nuanced internal deliberations ongoing in relation to religious and theological narratives.

Tandiwae described her own deliberations, saying, "I knew that I could not ever act upon my liking another woman. It was just something that would have to stay hidden within me." She continued to explain the connection to her religious family and community, saying,

And in order for me to have a way out, would be I would have to pack it down and, you know, there was no way out for me. In my mind, I couldn't come out because it would destroy my father's ministry. I couldn't come out because it would destroy my family accepting me. I would be rejected. And these are things I thought because of my Southern Baptist upbringing and all those things I had heard preached from the pulpit and the scriptures that I had learned. So there was no way out for me if I wanted to be accepted by the church, accepted by my family, and accepted in the public. There was no way I could come out. Because I didn't want to be alone out there. I didn't know how to do it.

Here, Eribon helpfully points to the power of insult and intimidation—religious or otherwise—in erecting boundaries between public and private life for an LGBTQ person. He argues,

It is, in fact, insult—its power of intimidation—that establishes the frontier between public and private for gays and lesbians. Thus the public and private spheres are not materially or physically distinct spaces for them (public being the street, work, politics; private being the home and personal relations). Rather it is a matter of a binary structure that reproduces itself in homologous fashion in every lived situation and in every social relation.[12]

Hearing anti-LGBTQ messages preached from the pulpit, compounded by the fear of rejection from family and church groups, helped to draw the boundaries between public and private life for Tandiwae in ways that defined the topography of the soul—keeping certain parts of her sense of self hidden within.

Thomas used bodily language to describe what parts of his life he felt the need to "hide" from others and the ways this kept him from learning about sexuality in the way that he imagined his straight peers were learning rather effortlessly. He surmised,

> And I think when you're close to other people—when you can be close to them—when you don't have to worry about, "Oh, there's this entire part of my body like from here down that you're not allowed to see. You can only look at this part. Let's only talk up here." If you don't have to do that then you can learn in subtle ways, you know, boys can teach each other how to deal with their feelings of sexuality. They just do it. They don't talk about it.

Eribon notes the public/private deliberations for gay men are imposed upon men and boys by the structures of oppression. He argues, "These structures define the contours of ways of being or ways of life that require a radical dissociation between one's hidden self and one's presentable self . . . public life is fundamentally linked to heterosexuality and excludes anything that deviates from it."[13] Again, the importance of a legitimizing audience for the narrative sources of our sense of self were lacking in Thomas' experience in ways that seemed obviously supplied in the lives of his straight male peers, marking parts of himself unacceptable for public expressions.

Juliana, an African American woman, helpfully drew together her experience as both a racial and sexual minority:

> I haven't talked too much about being an African American in this position, but it's part and parcel of all of it. So you have some idea of how to articulate your experience as a numerical minority—as a visible numerical minority. As one that is not so visible or it's in question or people look at you and wonder—that's a different thing. Or even further, having to hide what may be glaringly obvious. So you have to hide this thing that is obvious. How do you hide something that's obvious? So that kind of determined how I ran my life.

For Juliana, her sexual identity felt obvious to others looking on at her life, but she continued to attempt to hide what already felt obvious in ways that determined the trajectory of her life for many years leading up to her suicide attempt. Narrativally, Cobb illustrates the importance of the theme of feeling hidden within, again noting the need for an "audience" for legitimazing the narratives that shape our self-understandings. She argues that "we are legitimate as speakers not through the stories we tell ourselves about ourselves, but through the stories we tell <u>to others</u> about ourselves, stories that can then be elaborated by the interlocutors to materialize and anchor the speaker's legitimacy."[14]

This, too, is related to the concern of "narrative foreclosure" explored above, as narratives that that seem fundamental to self-understanding may be delegitimized and foreclosed upon when they have no outlet for expression within an audience of others who may receive and further elaborate these stories. In Brison's words, constructing self-narratives require an audience that is "able and willing to hear us and to understand our words as we intend them."[15] For most of these research participants, these audiences were unavailable and a significant part of their day-to-day experience of life was kept hidden within.

Juliana did draw on the metaphor of "the closet" to describe how this hiddenness affected her. She said, "The closet is a big deal because it just makes life very inconvenient, at the very least. It also is meant to chip away at your sense of self." The compulsory hiddenness is meant to "make you question your . . . relative humanity."

FEELING TRAPPED

Evident in Juliana's sense of "futility" and present in the narratives of many research participants, there emerged a sense that many participants felt trapped in their lives leading up to a suicide attempt. This is a valance of experience that is often lost in popular and clinical discourse addressing suicide experience among LGBTQ people. Yet it was a prominent component of the experience of subjective precarity for many of the participants in this study.

Kate, an evangelical Christian who continues to struggle intellectually and spiritually with questions of the acceptability of her same-sex attraction, described her sense of being trapped or stuck in these words:

> Regardless of whether I think it's a sin or not, I'm never going to be able to get rid of it. And so I think for me that was really depressing because I was like, I can't do anything about it so this affects my life— for the rest of my life it affects marriage, relationships, it'll affect a lot of things. And so I think that was kind of where I got a lot more depressed.

Though she has emerged from the intensity of her experience of depression and the suicidal thoughts that characterized much of her college years, she continues to experience a feeling of stuckness in relation to her ongoing religious questions and the embodiment of her sexuality. She continued,

> And part of the reason that I do want to kind of figure all of this out is I feel like being unsettled I don't know, sometimes I don't feel like I can really go forward. Sometimes I can—I feel like I can encourage people. But it'd be nice to have it down and know what I think and I can be like, okay . . . Knowing, okay, this is where I stand, would kind of help me to know how to make decisions and how to encourage people. Because if you're kind of like—I've held back some in certain situations just because I don't know where I stand.

This sense of feeling trapped or stuck seems distinct from the deliberations over public/private hiddenness and revelation, as this valence of experience seems determinative for many participants of the trajectory of their lives, rather than simply informing decisions over disclosure. In a further example, a friend in college asked Silas to finish the sentence, "Life is . . . " Silas responded, "Life is, therefore live. And live it with all your might. Kind of the carpe diem thing." I asked Silas how that personal philosophy changed to the point of trying to take her own life. She replied by telling the story of coming out to her mother who responded by punching her in the face. She continued,

> Well when my mother punched me in the face and I was only working part time, then I kind of felt that I was trapped and that, you know, I wasn't going to change . . . So I had given up. I gave up. I realized I wasn't going to be accepted here. My mother, I was going to be nothing but a disappointment to her and, you know, I just I really felt trapped.

This is a similar description to Juliana's when she said, "The more I run from this the more I run smack into it." For Silas, the feeling of being trapped seemed imbricated with the lack of "audience"—as treated above—for her own developing self-narratives in relation to her sexual identity, as well as to a lack of options in her life, now a college graduate and living back home with her mother.

Tandiwae, whose father was a minister and whose own vocational trajectory was directed toward ministry very early in her life, drew on this theme of feeling trapped or, in her words, having "no way out," and implicated the theological doublespeak treated in chapter three in bringing about this sense. She described the message she consistently received, saying,

> "For God so loved the world, he loves you, just don't act on it." And it's like, as I look back and think about those sermons, they really did impact me to the point of where I had no way out. I had no—I could not act upon what I really felt and it was really hard and it was getting harder. The older I became, it got harder.

This sense of feeling "trapped," stuck, or having "no way out" seems further related to the concept of narrative foreclosure that Freeman describes as "the conviction that the story of one's life, or life work, has effectively ended. At an extreme, narrative foreclosure may lead to a kind of living death or even suicide, the presumption being that the future is a foregone conclusion, an inevitable reiteration of one's present suffering or paralysis."[16] Cobb believes that when interpellation takes place to position persons in ways that are unfitting, it may result in the enactment of that lack of fit. She argues, "When identity or positions are problematic for people, they work to alter or reorganize those positions."[17] While not suggested in Cobb's research, my own research leads me to question whether suicide might be conceived as an enactment of a lack of narratival fit—especially when strong theological discourses position LGBTQ persons in ways that diminish the livability of life.

THE UNFINALIZABILITY OF LGBTQ SUICIDE EXPERIENCE

While the thematic development that I have performed here seems helpful in the understanding of LGBTQ suicide experience, I am very clear that in working at the intersection of this research data and the theoretical materials I am drawing upon, my thematic developments could take many, many different directions. These narratives are truly "unfinalizable." As Frank argues with dialogical narrative analysis, "Storytelling plays upon a tension between forces that would finalize lives and the imagination of life as unfinalized."[18] Just as I recognize the unfinalizable nature of these narratives in my own theoretical work, I also recognize this unfinalizability in the narrative habitus of the participants themselves.

I hear in these stories the interpellative potential of narratives to set life on edge, diminishing livability through feelings of internal unmooring, hiddenness, and a sense of being trapped and calling for certain narratival outcomes—in this case, death in a multivalent sense. But what I witnessed in the narratival renderings of these stories in the research interviews with these nine participants is a persistent resistance to this interpellation—participants devising methods to open new narrative pathways beyond narrative foreclosure and into a livable future. In the following chapter, I will turn analytical attention to the interview materials to develop constructive theological proposals for addressing experiences of subjective precarity and LGBTQ suicide.

NOTES

1. Arthur W. Frank, "Practicing Dialogical Narrative Analysis," in *Varieties of Narrative Analysis*, eds. James Holstein and Jaber F. Gubrium (Thousand Oaks, CA: SAGE, 2012), 49.

2. Hilde Lindemann Nelson, *Damaged Identities, Narrative Repair* (Ithaca, NY: Cornell University Press, 2001), 71.

3. Nelson, *Damaged Identities, Narrative Repair*, 99.

4. R.D. Laing, *The Divided Self: An Existential Study in Sanity and Madness* (Harmondsworth, UK: Penguin, 1960), 42.

5. Ian Burkitt, *Social Selves: Theories of Self and Society*, 2nd ed. (Los Angeles: SAGE, 2008), 76.

6. Judith Butler, *Precarious Life: The Powers of Mourning and Violence* (New York: Verso, 2004), 31.

7. Didier Eribon, *Insult and the Making of the Gay Self*, trans. Michael Lucey (Durham, NC: Duke University Press, 2004), 116.

8. Nelson, *Damaged Identities, Narrative Repair*, xii.

9. Burkitt, *Social Selves*, 76.

10. Mark Freeman, *Hindsight: The Promise and Peril of Looking Backward* (New York: Oxford University Press, 2010), 12.

11. Nelson, *Damaged Identities, Narrative Repair*, 101.

12. Eribon, *Insult and the Making of the Gay Self*, 104–5.

13. Eribon, *Insult and the Making of the Gay Self*, 104.

14. Sara Cobb, *Speaking of Violence: The Politics and Poetics of Narrative in Conflict Resolution* (New York: Oxford, 2013), 65. Emphasis in original.

15. Susan J. Brison, *Aftermath: Violence and the Remaking of a Self* (Princeton, NJ: Princeton University Press, 2002), 51.

16. Freeman, *Hindsight*, 125.

17. Cobb, *Speaking of Violence*, p. 218

18. Frank, "Practicing Dialogical Narrative Analysis," 45.

FIVE

Religious Resistance

Ernst Bloch argued, "The best thing about religion is that it makes for heretics."[1] LGBTQ people are no strangers to the accusations of heresy— living outside the restricting dictates of so much Christian teaching on sexuality and gender to the chagrin of many of the faith's teachers. For many throughout history, this persistent targeting for admonishment by faith leaders has led many LGBTQ people to leave churches and the Christian faith altogether. For others, however, there is much within the tradition that is too important to let go of entirely.

Entering this research process, I assumed that I would hear many stories of "rejecting religion," exiting communities of faith, and taking leave of church altogether. This assumption is, indeed, supported in the social science literature on LGBTQ religiosity.[2] While this suspicion was confirmed, what I did not expect was just where these religious departures would lead participants. I discovered in participants' stories a religious tenacity that defies popular imagination about the necessity of queer people to abandon church and leave religion behind. Participants described their lives with a greater degree of complexity than either the social science literature or popular media typically portray.

These forms of resistance and religious reconfiguration also played a major role in participants' sense of self. As Eribon notes,

> To decide that you are going to free your speech from the constraints imposed by permanent self-surveillance means not only that you have chosen to oppose an identity that has been imposed and hidden with one that has been chosen and affirmed. It also implies that you will have to reconstruct yourself and find the means and the support structures to enable such a transformation.[3]

As will become clear in the research data presented, participants navigated the experiences of theological interpellation and subjective precar-

77

ity addressed in the last chapter in ways that both refashioned their religious practices, but also reconstructed their deepest sense of self set within
an ultimate context. This work is reminiscent of what Judith Butler names
as the emergence of "critique," saying

> This is the juncture from which critique emerges, where critique is
> understood as an interrogation of the terms by which life is constrained
> in order to open up the possibility of different modes of living; in other
> words, not to celebrate difference as such but to establish more inclu-
> sive conditions for sheltering and maintaining life that resists models of
> assimilation.[4]

For many of the LGBTQ people in this study, the work of critique
emerged at critical junctures in their narratives in attempt to fend off
violence against a sense of "soul" that so many encountered in the religious communities of their upbringing.

As a reminder to readers, when I speak in metaphors of coreness,
rather than being an ontological and essentialized "reality" always and
already there resting in the "depths" of our being, a *sense* of our coreness
bespeaks the deeply constitutive narratives and operations of power/
knowledge intersecting our bodies to produce a perceptual *experience* and
narratival *sense* about who we are as human beings and how we are
situated in the world in relation to others and in relation to a presumed
ultimate context. In other words, I am interested in a *sense*, a *perception*,
and *interpretive event* that may, at times, present in metaphorical terms as
something that is "core" to who we are as human beings. "As stories tell
people who they are," Frank argues, "those people are embodied as
much by stories as by their flesh. Stories, like bodies and in symbiosis
with bodies, are people's dignity and their calamity."[5]

But as calamitous as the religious, spiritual, and theological narratives
have been up to this point in the exploration of participants' experience,
some strands of theological narrative also served to support the livability
of life in the aftermath of suicide attempt. Frank describes a central question of socionarratology that becomes imperative in this chapter: "How is
the storyteller holding his or her own in the act of storytelling?" By *holding one's own*, Frank is pointing to the ability of the storyteller "to sustain
the value of one's self or identity in response to whatever threatens to
diminish that self or identity."[6] The narratives of religious resistance and
the refashioning of religious practice described by participants in this
chapter bespeak each one's ability to "hold their own" amid the often
crushing discursive forces of theological narratives that attack their sense
of personhood in relation to others and in relation to a presumed ultimate
context, or "God."

In her own study of narratives of recovery after trauma and abuse,
philosopher Susan Brison employs the metaphor of soul to suggest that
the "study of trauma also replaces the traditional philosophical puzzle

about whether the soul can survive the death of the body with the question of whether the self can reconstitute itself after obliteration at the hands of another."[7] This is the question of "soul" that takes center stage in this chapter—how one's deepest sense of self can be reconstituted after near "obliteration."

I employed the metaphor of "subjective precarity" in the last chapter to indicate the many ways that discursive forms of violence operate upon the lives of these nine LGBTQ participants. In this chapter, I employ the metaphor of "subjective solidity," drawing on the thought of Czech philosopher Jan Patočka, to understand how these narratives point us toward solidity-producing acts and movements in the lives of participants. Findaly sees Patočka's philosophical stance of "thinking questioningly" as central to the production of "solidity." It is this "thinking questioningly"—the ability and willingness of participants to resist given "truths" and authoritative theological pronouncements and think "transgressively"—that seems to have produced a sense of subjective "solidity" in the aftermath of suicide attempt.

Findlay sees the production of solidity integrally related to Patočka's sense of what it means to care for souls. Findlay argues,

> The solidity achieved by caring for the soul consists neither of an objectively derived system based on material elements, nor of a simple, divine being on whom we can fall back when we are in doubt. It is, instead, a ground for our conduct based on the formation of our being, its unification, by the process that is most distinctly ours as human beings: the process of "thinking questioningly" that leads to understanding.[8]

Here we turn to the narratives of interviewees that are suggestive of the experience of increasing *subjective solidity*, accomplished through resistive acts of "thinking questioningly" and acting transgressively in the resistance to religious violence and the refashioning of spiritual practices.

I categorize the five prominent themes that point to the practice of "religious resistance" and the "refashioning of religious practice" in the lives of participants as: narratives of exodus and spiritual migration, revising theological frameworks, refashioning individual spiritual practices, developing altruistic spiritual practices, and embracing transgressive religious identity. I will further draw upon these themes to suggest how, in my research, the concept of "soul" is being re-visioned, pointing us to the development of practices of care that will be the focus of the final chapter.

NARRATIVES OF EXODUS AND SPIRITUAL MIGRATION

While social scientists often note the loss of religious or spiritual identity among LGBTQ people—one study of gay men suggesting a rejection level up to 69 percent for gay men[9]—a simple binary of acceptance/rejection is an uncritical perspective on the complexities of religious and spiritual engagement itself and an unnuanced understanding of LGBTQ experience with religion and spirituality more specifically. While outright "rejection" of religion may be descriptive of some LGBTQ persons' experience, my research participants displayed a wide range of strategies for the resistance of religions and spiritual discursive violence and the refashioning and reconfiguration of religious practice performed in service to the livability of life.

"Leaving church" or "rejecting religion" doesn't rightly portray the reality of those who were "left by" their churches. The nine research participants in my study, along with numerous other LGBTQ people, regularly experience messages of rejection from religious communities and outright denial of participation in the most important aspects of church life. While "rejecting religion" or "leaving church" doesn't quite capture the complexity of the situation for most, it seems important to recognize the agential activity indicated when "leaving" churches does occur.

My interviewees did not capitulate to the pressure to conform by rejecting one's own sense of same-sex attraction or transgender identity as "sinful" or "disordered," even when that pressure to conform takes the form of painful rejection. Rather, many participants described their exit from their faith communities as the beginning of a longer journey that they made with some intentionality, albeit under pressure. These journeys are an exodus, of sorts, spiritual migrations in search of more promising, life-affirming religious communities and spiritual practices.

In an extended excerpt from my interview with Tandiwae, she explained how an ecclesial distancing took place after she came out to her two communities of faith, both Southern Baptist churches she served in official lay-ministerial capacities working with the churches' youth and music ministries:

> **Tandiwae:** They didn't tell me I couldn't come back, but I stopped getting invited to a lot of things. So I just thought, you know what, screw it. I don't need church. I don't need religion. And I stopped going. I totally rejected all religion. Every religion. Anything there was out there, I refused to go.

> **Cody**: So when that occurred, you rejected religion and refused to go, did you still have some sense of your own spirituality?

> **Tandiwae:** I began saying, "Thank you God for creating me as you did. I know you created me. Now you've got to help me figure out how to live through this and who I am. What do I need to do?" I never rejected God. I never blamed God. I would always ask God, you

know, "How can this be? What did you do? How do I do this?" I
would ask a lot of questions of him. And I always knew that it was
okay to question God. It wasn't okay to condemn God, but questioning God was okay. And I would drive down the road and have full
conversations with God, you know? And I had total faith that I was
okay with who I was in his eyes. That he loved me for who I was
because he created me this way. And I got that. Then I started thinking, "Okay, so what do I do now God? Do I just live everyday and just
be who I am and be okay and I don't have to go to church? I don't
have to be involved?" And for somebody who's been involved in
church for forty years, you know, it was hard to not go, to not open
that Bible. I even refused to open the Bible. It was like, "You know
God, it's not that I'm mad at you, I'm just mad at everything that's
around me."

This piece of Tandiwae's narrative is illustrative of the ways that "rejecting religion" doesn't equate to the rejection of one's prior religious
beliefs (e.g., her belief in a God who created her and cares for her life and
wellbeing) and spiritual practices (e.g., her practice of praying to God).
These elements of her religious and spiritual life maintain a place of
central importance in Tandiwae's spiritual journey after the rejection of
her religious communities.

While her decision seems simple and her breaks with her former
churches seem straightforward and clean, it was far from easy for Tandiwae to separate from these communities of faith. She described the ways
that her physical presence in the church buildings was an important part
of her faith practice, saying, "I had to be outside of those buildings looking in going, 'I should be able to be in there but they won't let me in there
because I'm different!'" Through this experience of rejection and leaving
her former Southern Baptist churches, she began to discover that she no
longer needed to be in these buildings on a regular basis in order to
experience "the presence of God"—a theological shift she considers a
marker of growth in her own spirituality.

While some, like Tandiwae, received messages of overt rejection after
outing herself to her faith communities, Florence received no direct pressure to conform to a heterosexual ideal or any direct rejection from her
religious communities, as she had never disclosed her same-sex attraction to anyone in her life. Her sense of need to distance herself from her
religious beliefs and commitments in order to pursue a relationship with
another woman came from ambient messages of incompatibility between
a lesbian identity and Christian faith. She explains the moment when she
made a clear decision between the two, saying,

> So, I had made a conscious decision that I was going to pursue a rela-
> tionship or pursue some sort of sexual intimacy with my friend. And in

making that conscious decision had sort of decided that it was okay for me to let go of my religious beliefs. So I was kind of in that space of having decided that this was worth pursuing and that it would be alright if I didn't have faith anymore. And I hadn't really talked to anybody about it. This was just sort of in my own sensibility about myself . . . and I kind of had that conversation with God, like, "I'm going to leave now. See you later. We're done. Thank you." I really had had that kind of prayer conversation saying, "I'm done with you. If this is what you really think, I'm done with you." So I felt like that relationship was gone. I knew my parents . . . my family would not be supportive. All of the things that sort of anchored me to life just crumbled.

This excerpt from Florence further exemplifies the ways that the discursive paradigm of a simple, dichotomous acceptance/rejection of religion is clearly untenable for understanding the imbrication between religion and spiritual identity and sexual/gender identity for many LGBTQ people. For Florence, who eventually returned to Christianity and made several denominational movements to increasingly more liberal denominational bodies and entered a vocation in Christian ministry and scholarship, her religious and spiritual identity felt deeply connected to a sense of "anchoring" in life. Forfeiting these "anchors," coupled with the romantic rejection she experienced from her friend, produced a sense of precarity leading to her first and only suicide attempt. Clearly, however, abandoning hope of a fulfilling relationship with another women was also an option that seemed out of the question—so much so that briefly abandoning her religious moorings seemed necessary.

After an initial period of distress and unrest that included his attempt at suicide, Thomas began to make his own deliberations about his involvement in his conservative Christian faith tradition. He describes the decision he reached—transcending the binary of acceptance/rejection of religion—this way:

I became calm enough to realize that I would rather jettison the teachings that I'd been given about God, and Christ, and the Holy Spirit, and the Kingdom of God and hold onto my faith in Christ. And if it meant that I never had a community ever again, fuck it. I will just take it. Because my faith is more important. My faith is the only thing. I couldn't explain it.

Thomas was very articulate about the development of his theological perspectives and his search for a community of faith in which these theological perspectives may find a fit alongside his sexual identity. His forfeiting of religious *community* for the sake of a personal *faith* in Christ further complexifies the acceptance/rejection of religion binary in relation to LGBTQ lives, bespeaking a religious "exodus" or spiritual migration undertaken with less certainty about the destination of the journey. Though he has struggled for years to find such a community with little success, he exhibits an air of defiance and theological fortitude in the face of those who continue to deny the compatibility of his religious faith and sexual identity, saying.

> Marching in a gay pride parade where somebody says, "Your going to go to hell because you're gay." And [I] would think, you know, I believe in the Lord. If he wants to put me in hell, that's where I should go! I don't give a shit. It's God's business. Let's not think about this anymore . . . So that was me beginning to divorce from old traditions.

While a "divorce from old traditions" was suitable for Thomas and led to the development of a robust, reflective perspective on faith and religious practice, Silas explained to me the tension experienced between wishing to retain the conservative religious beliefs and communities forming Silas's adolescence and young adulthood and the desire to be accepted and embraced by these communities in the fullness of Silas's sexual and gender identities. Having tried more liberal, LGBTQ-affirming faith communities, Silas remains unsatisfied with the "fit" of these churches to Silas's own faith commitments, beliefs, and practices.

Silas says, "What I wanted, I guess, was my cake and eat it too. I wanted to be able to have the religion and beliefs and thoughts that we had and I had, and I wanted to be able to marry the woman of my choice." Describing this struggle, Silas muses, "I would have been better off being an atheist and having good morals than a condemned Christian. That's the conclusion I've come to." Now, decades from her suicide experience, Silas continues to struggle with the lack of acceptance in the faith communities to which Silas most wishes to belong and a dissatisfaction with the faith communities to which Silas *could* belong as a lesbian and gender queer person. Yet, Silas continues to struggle with what it means to live by the moral principles that Silas cherishes, all the while removed from the supportive presence of a faith community.

REVISING THEOLOGICAL FRAMEWORKS

Evident by now is the fact that the "exoduses" and "spiritual migrations" these participants made from many of their original faith communities are not simply a "leaving" of a particular church or faith community, but an exodus journey in a larger sense. Each participant portrayed a journey of difficulty, exploration, discovery, and uncertainty that sometimes led to joining new communities of faith and sometimes led to developing other methods of spiritual practice outside of traditional, organized faith communities. But, *in every case*, the exodus journey led participants to revised theological frameworks and religious/spiritual understandings, making participants, at times, "transgressive theologians" for the livability of their own lives.

Edward Findlay draws upon the philosophy of Jan Patočka in ways that illuminate the experiences exhibited in the narratives of these nine participants and that will also inform my own continued exploration of the metaphor, "soul," in relation to these findings. Findlay says,

> We are all confronted, at some point in our lives, with situations in which our simple beliefs, our self-evident understandings, are shattered. "Those experiences, which show us that this whole way of seeing the world as self-evident and assumed is something that disappoints, something open to negative outcomes, these experiences are rare; they are rare but, in the end, everyone encounters them in some way or another." It is not the encounter with such experience, of course, that is crucial; it is our response to the encounter that marks the decisive movement.[10]

So too, many LGBTQ people encounter situations, like those of my participants, through which "simple beliefs" and "self-evident understandings" are shattered. Patočka and Findlay are pointing toward a more foundational philosophical situation that leads to a shattering of the simply given meanings of metaphysical grand narratives. The "shattering" that occurs for participants, however, range from the shattering of simple religious beliefs or trust in religious authorities that seem no longer tenable in light of lived human experience to far more comprehensive philosophical and theological shifts in framework that approach the type of philosophical shattering Patočka and Findlay suggest, rearranging the entirety of one's life.

While some participants like Kate and Matthew moved from churches and universities that taught the sinfulness of homosexuality to find churches, friends, communities, and educational institutions more embracing of their same-sex sexual identities, others, like Juliana, made larger philosophical and theological shifts. Juliana was raised in a conservative African American Protestant denomination and attended a fundamentalist, Pentecostal university. She described the way the simple beliefs and self-evident understandings surrounding sexuality led to more extensive revising of theological frameworks. She says, "There have been times when I've thought that the gay thing made it easy. Because that's one really obvious thing that you can point to that's like the broken cog in a wheel that doesn't allow the wheel to turn anymore."

These narratives move us from experiences of "shattering" and the production of subjective precarity into the production of some form of subjective "solidity" through the refashioning of theological and spiritual narratives that help participants "hold their own."[11] Chapters 3 and 4 illuminated many of the ways that some theological narratives can become dangerous to LGBTQ persons, provoking vulnerability and a precarious subjectivity leading to suicide attempt. We now turn to the ways participants form, deform, and reform narratives in order to "hold their own" in life.

Here, a pragmatist theological approach to theology's *telos* iterated by Gordon Kaufman guides in an understanding of these shifting theological perspectives. Kaufman argues,

> Theology, however, is not so much devotion to the symbols of faith as the attempt to *understand* those symbols and the way they function in human life, to criticize and reinterpret them so they will more adequately achieve their purpose, and finally . . . to reconstruct them, sometimes radically . . . It is a *deliberate human activity* directed toward criticizing and reconstructing the symbols by which faith lives and to which faith responds. [12]

Given this operative understanding of theology undergirding this work, I must emphasize that the *"deliberative human activity* directed toward criticizing and reconstructing the symbols by which faith lives" is the very work that these nine participants are doing in their own lives, responding with resistance to theological symbols that no longer facilitate the livability of life and often work to *diminish* that livability.

One important question is *how* these theological frameworks began to shift toward frameworks that provide the narrative material to "hold one's own" and sustain the livability of life. For Tandiwae, as for several participants, the process involved being introduced to LGBTQ-affirming theological reading materials that opened new possibilities of theological imagination. She describes an ex-girlfriend giving her a copy of Mel White's memoir, *Stranger at the Gate*,[13] which began prompting major theological shifts in her perspective:

> So I took that book home with me and . . . I didn't come out for a day and a half and I read that entire book. Balled my head open. Thanked God and realized I was created this way. Mel White helped me understand that I'm not something strange that I chose. I was created this way. This is who he wanted me to be. My being was my ministry. And like, oh wow, okay. So life started changing for me then. I actually started going, okay, I'm okay. I am okay. But I still knew I couldn't come out yet.

Later, Tandiwae and her significant other discovered a meeting of gay evangelical Christians and decided to attend the conference. This proved to be an equally significant encounter for Tandiwae that provided further community support and increased the theological possibilities for reworking her theological self-understanding.

This excerpt from Tandiwae's story is illustrative of Frank's argument when he says, "The primary resources for telling a new story are the stories that are already circulating in the setting."[14] While this proved to be a significant turning point in Tandiwae's life, increasing possibilities for her own livability and opening new pathways to spiritual practice,

the beginning of this process was a slight reworking of already circulating theological narratives. It began with reworking a narrative of oneself
as a creation of God by incorporating an understanding of oneself created
as a lesbian.

Similarly, Kate's reworking of already circulating theological narratives hinged upon narratives of God's love for her. After a period of
religious distancing during which she no longer practiced her regular
reading of the Bible, she felt something significant missing from her life
and returned to a regular practice of devotional Bible reading. She describes this return, saying,

> So I started spending more time in [God's] word and realizing that he
> did love me. And he's always loved me, but I think in that mentality—
> the mindset I had before I think was really affected by my environ-
> ment. And I think being out of that environment and seeing positivity
> around me and then just spending time in God's word, being like,
> okay, God does love me and I was looking at this wrong. I think just
> revisiting the gospel, what it means to be in Christ and what that looks
> like, was really important for me. So I think just like rekindling that
> relationship with him. And I'm still kind of not really close to him like
> where I feel that it should be. But I don't hate him anymore . . . Just
> going through the Bible and trying to figure out—it's actually really
> reopened a lot of things for me.

But, like Juliana above, sexuality served for Kate as "the broken cog in a
wheel that doesn't allow the wheel to turn anymore"—at least not as
effortlessly and unquestioningly as it turned before. Beyond reworking a
theological narrative about God's love for her, this broken cog also
prompted other shifts in Kate's theological framework, beyond revised
understanding of sexuality. She explains, "So I think it's opened my eyes
to a lot of things, not just sexuality, but a lot of different things in God's
word. It's just easy to kind of grow up hearing something, reading something, even creation and things like that."

Making this shift in theological framework, alongside finding more
affirming community outside of her fundamentalist Christian university,
allowed Kate's experience as lesbian to align with a greater degree of
congruence with her evangelical Christian theology. She said,

> I just think the spiritual aspect has a huge effect. But as well as it being
> damaging, I think it was also very healing as well through the process.
> Because, like, once I realized that my view of God was wrong and that I
> was projecting other people's opinions on him, and then going back to
> God's word and realizing that he died for me, he loves me, he's my
> father. And experiencing non-judgment from other people, other
> Christians—that was very restorative to my soul.

For Miguel, the journey toward revising theological frameworks took
on an intentional and methodical progression that spanned two of his

teenage years. He selected every major religion and spiritual practice he knew to explore and spent two weeks investigating each religion, speaking to two leaders within the particular religious group, attempting to fully practice that religious tradition for the two week span of time, asking several questions of each group: "Does it contradict itself? What is the philosophy? What are the principles? Do they make sense compared to what reality is?" During this lengthy span of religious investigation, Miguel committed that he could not kill himself or hurt any living creature and prayed, "God, at some point if I miss you, if I go through all this and I miss you somewhere, you have to give me something that's going to linger and stay there long enough to find out if this is true." After exploring Buddhism, Eastern philosophy, Mormonism, the spiritual use of crystals, Satanism, paganism, witchcraft, etc., Miguel—who grew up nominally Catholic—eventually decided to become Protestant Christian.

While Miguel and many others in the study made spiritual migrations from one Christian church or denomination to another, Louise was one of only two participants in my study—the other being Juliana—making a more critical break with the Christian theology of their upbring. For Juliana, this takes the form of a more scholarly critique of Christianity and a turn toward Buddhism and mediation. Louise, whose critique is not informed by the formal theological education Juliana received, refashioned her belief in God in a way that she identifies as explicitly for the purposes of recovering from much of the constitutive violence she experienced earlier in her life. She explains,

> And even more than that—and this surprises people a lot—but I, maybe I just don't explain it well, but the idea, the fact that I don't believe in a God that says, "This is right and this is wrong and you're okay, but you're not and I don't like you but you're fine." The fact that I kind of got rid of that, in my mind anyway, and was like, okay I'm just going to say if there is a God, then God doesn't care. God doesn't care. I don't care, there's not enough to life or whatever. And people are like, "Don't you find that discomforting? Is that scary to think that we're just bacteria on a speck of dust in the universe?" I'm like, "No, it's so comforting because it means that whatever decisions I make aren't going to change the, you know, I can feel accepted in myself and not have to, like, be worried about somebody watching me" . . . it's just comforting. I don't know. Whether it be true or not, it's just a choice. It's almost like I've chosen to believe that because that's what I find comforting.

Finally, it is not only the typically understood "damning" and "damaging" theological understandings that are contested by participants. Juliana, whose own background includes extensive graduate theological education, goes so far as to contest the terms on which much LGBTQ-affirming theologies are based.

Juliana: So now the liberal take on LGBT souls is that God loves everyone. God loves all of God's children. So that, personally, that doesn't work for me either because I don't accept a Christian theology around it. It doesn't really speak to me and it didn't in 2000. Or 2001. Since then, how it speaks to me personally, I have to say it still doesn't but I don't have the strong reaction to it that I once did. And that may come from being a survivor.

Cody: You're talking about that strong reaction to the notion that God loves all LGBT people?

Juliana: Or the need to say that. Where that comes from. Where the need to say, well God loves me too. Or my soul is worth saving too. I too will go to Heaven. I used to have a very strong reaction to that whole thing and now it's kind of like, with my mom, if that's what works, well good. Good. Glad you found that.

Kaufman argues that theological "categories and concepts have been created in the efforts of men and women to grasp and comprehend their developing experience, and they have meaning only so far as they succeed in forming and interpreting experience."[15] It is especially the ability of these theological categories and concepts to deal with "the new, the unexpected, the startling" that proves the ultimate test of their viability and significance. Lived experience with the categories and concepts, according to Kaufman, "is the final court of appeal for all theological work . . . to see whether these can still make sense of our lives."[16] In the experience of these participants, the "final court of appeal" for their operative theological framework is the livability of life set within the ultimate context of these categories and concepts. For every participant, the development of new ways of theological grasping and comprehending their lived experience seemed necessary and they each became skillful theologians toward the livability of life in order to resist the violence of theological narratives and preserve a sense of connection to what they deemed of ultimate significance.

NOTES

1. Ernst Bloch, *Atheism in Christianity*, trans. J. T. Swann (New York: Verso, 1972), epigraph page.

2. Andrew William Wood and Abigail Holland Conley, "Loss of Religious or Spiritual Identity Among the LGBT Population," *Counseling and Values* 59 (2014): 95–111.

3. Didier Eribon, *Insult and the Making of the Gay Self*, trans. Michael Lucey (Durham, NC: Duke University Press, 2004), 101.

4. Judith Butler, *Undoing Gender* (New York: Routledge, 2004), 4.

5. Arthur W. Frank, *Letting Stories Breathe: A Socio-Narratology* (Chicago: University of Chicago, 2010), 146.

6. Arthur W. Frank, "Practicing Dialogical Narrative Analysis," in *Varieties of Narrative Analysis*, ed. James Holstein and Jaber F. Gubrium (Thousand Oaks, CA: SAGE, 2012), 33.

7. Susan J. Brison, *Aftermath: Violence and the Remaking of a Self* (Princeton, NJ: Princeton University Press, 2002), 45.

8. Edward F. Findlay, *Caring for the Soul in a Postmodern Age: Politics and Phenomenology in the Though of Jan Patočka* (Albany, NY: State University of New York Press, 2002), 67–68.

9. Glenn J. Wagner, James Serafini, Judith Rabkin, Robert Remien, and Janet Williams, "Integration of one's religion and homosexuality: A weapon against internalized homophobia?," *Journal of Homosexuality* 26 (1994): 91–110.

10. Findlay, *Caring for the Soul in a Postmodern Age*, 104–5.

11. Recall Frank's questions guiding socionarratological inquiry drawn upon here: "Who uses a story to hold their own, and how the story does that, are crucial questions. But it must always be complemented by the questions of whom the story renders vulnerable; who now has an increased problem of holding their own, once the story has been told?" Frank, *Letting Stories Breathe*, 78.

12. Gordon D. Kaufman, *An Essay on Theological Method*, 3rd ed. (Atlanta, GA: Scholars Press, 1995), xx.

13. Mel White, *Stranger at the Gate: To Be Gay and Christian in America* (New York: Plume, 1995).

14. Frank, "Practicing Dialogical Narrative Analysis," 44.

15. Kaufman, *An Essay on Theological Method*, 10.

16. Kaufman, *An Essay on Theological Method*, 10.

SIX

Holding One's Own

In addition to the ways that queer souls experience a solidification against precarity-inducing religious and theological narratives through undertaking exoduses and spiritual migrations, as well as revising theological frameworks toward the project of survival, there are also strategies that participants developed to "hold their own" against the soul violence inflected by the uptake of these narratives from the collective library into the inner library. Three such strategies that bore similarity across many of the participant's interviews were projects of refashioning their individual spiritual practices, developing altruistic spiritual practices, and embracing a transgressive religious identity.

REFASHIONING INDIVIDUAL SPIRITUAL PRACTICES

In addition to the revision of theological frameworks and ways of *thinking* about life set within an ultimate context, the experience of subjective precarity and the "shattering experiences" of participants also became sites of resistance. This resistance took shape through experiences allowing for more mobility, flexibility, and change in one's religious/spiritual engagement and *practice*. Though I did not ask specific questions to the interviewees about the development of their individual spiritual practices, these practices used by participants to sustain their sense of religious identity or spirituality continued to come up in many of the interviews.

These individual spiritual practices are indicative of participants' strategies of resistance to the constitutive violence and damaging theological interpellation and seem to serve as methods of either reclaiming something of importance from their religious heritage or developing new, sustaining spiritual practices. This refashioning of individual spiritual practices speak to Foucault's description of resistance as "playing the same game differently, or playing another game, another hand, with other trump cards."[1] Often the same religious language, imagery, and practice that perpetrated violence against their senses of soul were drawn upon differently for the project of survival.

For Thomas, a significant shift occurred in his approach to theological issues. There was a shift away from the answers and certainty that were used in life-diminishing ways throughout his childhood, and toward a foregrounding of God's love and acceptance and an embrace of uncertainty in matters Thomas felt to be theologically non-essential. At the time of the interview, Thomas continues to practice Christianity within more liberal, mainline congregations and described to me the place that the spiritual practice of Bible reading continues to play in his religious experience. He stated,

> The Bible is wonderful. I love the whole thing. I mean . . . it makes me uncomfortable to read some of it, but, it's beautiful. I don't understand it in a linear way. And it's helps me. It's like a Boy Scout backpack or something, you know, I carry it around with me wherever I go and a wonderful scripture will help me in my life.

Thus, Thomas has augmented his understanding of the Bible and it's use by religious groups in ways that allow him to find comfort and spiritual encouragement in the very same text that was regularly used to denigrate him as a gay man.

Similarly, Tandiwae also maintains parts of the spiritual practices of her Southern Baptist upbringing, especially relying upon prayer in order to sense her own connection to God. After the period of her life when she was kicked out of her churches and contemplated suicide, she used prayer as a practice of speaking to God in ways that helped her cope with the pain of these experiences. She says, "My personal connection to God was that I knew I could talk to him and I knew that I could scream at him if I needed to and he'd be okay with me and love me."

In addition to drawing upon the same spiritual practices differently in resistance to their previous precarity-inducing power and in service to life's livability, some participants also developed new individual spiritual practices. Once she was cut off from the Christian communities of her upbringing, and after attaining a degree of stability in her own life, Tandiwae took up the spiritual practice of drumming. She describes the place of this practice in her life, saying, "Now, I'm an empowerment drummer. Now I use the drum and . . . if I'm hitting that beat, that rhythm, it's like that rhythm and my spiritual world is in a total connection. I would have never thought that as a Christian girl in the Southern Baptist church." While this is a new practice, it is also connected to Tandiwae's previous service as a music director in the Southern Baptist churches from which she was expelled after coming out.

Both before and after her suicide attempt and exodus from the denomination of her upbringing, Florence experienced singing as a central spiritual practice. She explains, "I was a singer and I sang in the choir. And it was probably the primary way I felt spiritual connection. Even when things were horrible, that was the one place I felt like maybe I still had a relationship with God." Florence described a period of time after her suicide attempt when she realized that her sense of having a "rotten core" was not necessarily the case, saying, "It really started to kind of gradually penetrate me that this wasn't necessarily a conflict [between lesbian sexuality and Christian faith]. Like it didn't have to be a rotten core and a good façade. That it really could be a good core." When I asked Florence what went into changing this sense she had about herself, she described a season in her university choir during which she had an important solo in a religious song. She continued,

> After our concert, the director came up to me and said, "I think the reason you're so good at singing this is because you really believe it and it just radiates out from the inside of you when you sing." And that was I think that point I thought there is something in me that's not just rotten—that there is maybe light in there. And it was kind of the affirmation of others that who I was came through in what I was doing—that it wasn't just, it wasn't really a façade and I could really believe that was part of who I was.

Florence continues to find singing an important spiritual practice that helps her to find "that intimacy with God that comes through music."

But in addition to singing, Florence was introduced to Buddhism and practices of meditation through her involvement in a Catholic religious order. Buddhist practice now also provides Florence an important source of spiritual connection to the Divine. She named her sense when practicing meditation as "swimming in the spirit," which she describes as a feeling of being "immersed in God's presence." Similarly, Buddhism has aided Juliana and the practice of meditation has helped in unexpected ways to cope with her experiences following her suicide attempt. Though Florence continues, at times, to deal with the reemergence of LGBTQ-denigrating spiritual narratives in her life, her spiritual practices operate as forms of resistance to violent theological narratives. She describes their effect saying, "And so coming back to that to remind myself that that connection is there and *that* story is not *my* story."

For other participants there seemed a greater desire for distance between the religious environment of their upbringing and the practices currently drawn upon in their spiritual lives. Louise, raised Catholic, went through a period of rejecting organized religion and practice altogether, but has since reengaged spiritual exploration. She explains this experience, saying,

And then once I started feeling more secure and grounded, I kind of started exploring the idea of spirituality again. And because I so furiously rejected organized religion, I misunderstood that to be an extension of spirituality, while they're not really the same things. And so I guess a big thing that changed it, actually, was that I started going to yoga a lot, which doesn't sound very spiritual but the place where I go, where I practice yoga is like high energy, or high spirit, like everybody's very kind and warm and they all talk about spirituality a lot and they all, like, it's just such an accepting environment. Like, more accepting than I've—I've just never been in a place like that where I literally, like, I feel like if I walked around naked people wouldn't be mad at me—that's how accepting it is.

While some would not immediately think of a yoga studio as a site of "organized religion," for Louise, it takes on many of the qualities of religious community centered on common spiritual practice. In this way, it serves for Louise as a spiritual practice that is restorative to her sense of connectedness to something transcendent—albeit not a transcendent deity, but transcendence toward other human beings and toward nature as a whole.

DEVELOPING ALTRUISTIC-COLLECTIVIST SPIRITUAL PRACTICES

Entering the research interviews, I carried many assumptions about the way that religious and spiritual narratives operate violently upon an LGBTQ person's deepest sense of self, or soul. Though I had few preconceived notions about how participants *resisted* this violence and narratively reconstitute their religious practices and self-understandings in the aftermath of the experience of subjective precarity leading to suicide attempt. One theme that surprised me in its consistency across the interviews and the strength with which participants foregrounded its importance is the theme I term the development of altruistic-collectivist spiritual practices. The distinction between these and the above "individual spiritual practices" hinges upon the *telos* of the practice, bespeaking the *directionality* of these practices and the hopes that participants had for the *effects* of these practices on the lives and wellbeing of others. That is, altruistic spiritual practices have in view not only the connection between an individual and the individual's sense of the Divine, but also—and perhaps *primarily*—the individual's connection to others.

I return here to Louise, who illustrates a turn toward altruistic spiritual commitments with rich and evocative language. Louise details the time when her perception of "spirituality" began to shift from an individualist to a collectivist/altruistic understanding, upon meeting a man whose Christian faith led him to live minimally and with the wellbeing of others in view. She explains how this meeting affected her, saying,

How he lives in a van and he lives minimally because we shouldn't need material things and we should feel, we should like, we should need nature and we should need each other and that was like, opened that collectivist view too. And that kind of made me feel much better about religion in general and that was sort of when I stopped being so angry. I mean, not when. It wasn't that moment. But that helped me to stop being so angry at the church and at religion because I was able to understand that, like, a group of people are not a religion. Right? Or not a spirituality or a belief.

Louise also identified the pressure she felt to identify her sexuality as an isolating experience from her sense of connection to others. She states that when she began identifying as bisexual, she felt dishonest to herself because of the limitation of this descriptor in relation to her sense of sexuality (she now identifies as pansexual). She explained, "And the more that I identified and put myself in these, like, narrow boxes of identifying whatever, the further I was from spirituality . . . and I don't even mean spirituality in the sense of a deity, but spirituality in the sense of oneness with the rest the world. And I just became so disconnected from everybody and from everything. And it just made everything worse."

A turn toward a collectivist and altruistic spiritual view had profound implications both for how Louise experienced her own sexuality and ability to self-identify in socially sanctioned terms, alongside her perspectives on religion more broadly. But beyond the revision of Louise's conception of spirituality and the decrease in her anger toward religion, what most intrigued me about her shift toward an altruistic spirituality is the ethical valance this practice takes on.

Judith Butler argues, "One insight that injury affords is that there are others out there on whom my life depends, people I do not know and may never know. This fundamental dependency on anonymous others is not a condition that I can will away."[2] It is a growing appreciation for this fundamental dependency, this dependency of one's life upon the lives of others, which seems to have grown out of Louise's painful and emotionally tumultuous experience in childhood and adolescence. She describes how awakening to this fundamental dependency now shapes her perspective upon her own subjectivity, saying,

I feel pain because they're feeling pain and that was sort of like okay, so maybe our sense of self—maybe individualness is not as important as, like, being collective and being kind of, not supernaturally, not even in like the mystical sense of it, but in the active sense of it. It's easier for me to discover my sense of self when I am being with other people, interacting with others, and trying to understand empathy and trying to, like, let them know that I'm feeling for them because it's helpful to know that you're not by yourself and you're not alone. And I think that whole individual self as soul, I am my special little snowflake, makes

you feel more disconnected. It makes it so much harder to feel you
have a place in the world because you have to find what place in the
puzzle, where are you, what piece are you? And that's just like way
overwhelming . . . And I more understand, like, it's easier to come to
terms with your own emotions when you realize that others are also
experiencing the same thing and it's not an individual experience. Especially pain. I think I feel like pain is much more collective.

It is important to recognize the way that this sense of spiritual, altruistic
collectivism emerged specifically out of her sense of pain and her ability
to connect this subjective sense of pain *intersubjectivly* to the pain of others. This speaks clearly to Butler's "insight that injury affords . . . that
there are others out there on whom my life depends" and, conversely,
others who are depending on me.

Though not conveyed in the same clear collectivist terms that Louise
expressed, Thomas expressed an ethical commitment to collectivist wellbeing throughout his interview. He railed against the privileging of theological "understandings" above the wellbeing of human lives affected
that he has observed and experienced in many ecclesial contexts. He
expressed a commitment to continually revising his own theological
framework and religious practices in view of an ethic of care for the lives
of others whose wellbeing may be otherwise diminished by specific theological frameworks. In this way, Thomas iterates his altruistic-collectivist
theological commitments, saying,

Now I'm in a position where I don't want the kingdom to come some-
time in the future anymore. I want it to be right here, right now.
Wherever we are, with whomever we're working . . . It's a life choice. I
want to do this on purpose now. I don't want to plan as if the kingdom
is some time far out. I don't want to plan as if God is going to save us
someday. I think he already did it. And we just help people live
through it.

Other participants told stories of concrete acts of commitment to altruistic-collectivist spiritual practices, directed toward cultivating the wellbeing of others. For example, advocacy for LGBTQ people became a
prominent theme in the lives of Florence, Tandiwae, and Silas. Florence
developed a clear connection between this LGBTQ advocacy work as a
spiritual practice emerging from her own theological commitments. She
explains,

The end of my sophomore year, my junior year of college I got really
involved in the Gay and Lesbian Alliance that was on campus. And
there was something really powerful to me about advocating for LGBT
folks on campus. So I think it connected me back to this sort of trans-
gressiveness of the church that I grew up in in that sense that—that
really Calvinist sense—that if the world is not the way that it is supposed to be then part of our job as Christians is to make it the way it is

supposed to be. To continue to live into that, that sense of God's realm present on earth. For me working with [the Gay and Lesbian Alliance] was—it became real to me that that work was part of Christian service. Like, I could imagine that the advocacy that I was doing was actually part of making the world the way it's supposed to be.

Similarly, Tandiwae prefaced her description of involvement in LGBTQ advocacy with the statement, "I am *being* more than I've ever been." She uses the metaphor of an eagle soaring to describe the development of her life trajectory since coming out to her family, exiting her Southern Baptist churches, and partnering with another woman. After describing her own sense of "soaring" in life, she poignantly stated, "I don't want to just soar to the point of where I'm alone out there and I'm living now. I want to soar with the strength of being able to help others along the way." She goes on to describe the way this desire to help others along the way relates to her own experience, in Butler's words, of the "insight that injury affords." She states,

> I don't want anyone else to live in that closet like that. I don't want anyone else to have to have those thoughts of suicide anymore. There's hope. And I want to, like, help see all these other people soar. I want to help them maneuver away from the closet and walk out and say, "Hey, you're not alone. You're okay." So what does it mean? To be fully alive. To embrace life. To embrace others who have gone through this journey and those who are looking at this going, "I'm at this beginning stage. What do I do? Do I go this route and suicide? Or this route where hopefully somebody's going to be there for me?"

This commitment to using one's own experience to help other LGBTQ people in similar situations arose time and again across all of my interview participants. It was the primary motivation that most had for involvement in the research in the first place.

Even beyond helping other LGBTQ people, participants expressed a wider commitment to helping others through situations of subjective precarity and suicide ideation more broadly. Kate described the way her own experience "opened up other venues" for helping others, providing this example:

> I was talking to a girl who had been sexually abused as a child and she goes through a lot of suicidal thoughts. So even though we went through different things—she's not gay and she's not struggling with that kind of thing—but just the hardships that she's been through. And then just being able to be like, you know, it's okay. People go through these hard times and how can I be here for you because I know what that feels like. So I think, really, it's helped me in my view of other people and the different struggles they've been through.

The development of collectivist spiritual practices enacted toward the cultivation of the wellbeing of others emerged as a primary theme in participants' theological frameworks and spiritual practices in the aftermath of their suicide attempt. This is akin to what Kaufman understands as the purpose of theological construction in a pragmatist vein. He suggests that this purpose "is to produce concepts (and world-pictures and stories) which make possible adequate orientation in life and the world." He continues,

> Of proposed concepts of God and world, therefore, one must ask such questions as these: What forms of human life do these conceptions of its context facilitate? Which forms inhibit? What possibilities do they open up for men and women? Which do they close off? . . . [T]he concepts of God and world must be assessed and reconstructed in consideration of the kinds of activity and forms of experience they make possible, rather than with referenced to some objects to which they are supposed to "correspond."[3]

Both for pragmatist theology and in the operative theologies of many of my participants, the ultimate criteria for the "success" or usefulness of theological constructions is not whether they correspond to the Truth of "how things are" in the world or with God, but in their ability to provide a map that "enables us to get where we are trying to go."[4] For participants, where they are trying to "go" is an exodus journey toward the fundamental livability of life—both their own and others. And in order to get there, they often became skillful "transgressive" theologians.

EMBRACING TRANSGRESSIVE RELIGIOUS IDENTITY

I noted in the interviews the tendency for religious communities and leaders to label participants as "transgressive" at the intersection of their faith practice and their sexual or gender identity. While these messages were intended to harm and were often experienced as painful and condemnatory by participants when they first occurred, it became evident that many of the participants intentionally *lived into* these transgressive religious identities in ways that contributed to their revision of theological frameworks and refashioning of religious practice toward the livability of life.

Eribon addresses the place of insult in the life of gay men, arguing, "To choose to be what you are can attenuate or annul the weight of 'deviance' that is lived as a personal drama. The recomposition of one's own subjectivity . . . can help to efface the heavy sense of fate."[5] Embracing the "transgressive" identities thrust upon them served as a type of "resistance" to the discursive forms of violence that operate at the constitutive and interpellative levels, which produce the sense of subjective precarity described in earlier chapters.

Foucault describes the way that resistance "always relies upon the situation against which it struggles."[6] In the case of these participants, the "resistance" practiced as "transgressive" theologians and creative practitioners of life-enabling spirituality often relied upon the religious context originally contributing to the precarity of participants. Rather than a theological framework or spiritual practices that were completely "new," many participants embraced aspects of their religious traditions and made critical shifts in how these religious components were believed or practiced, sometimes augmenting them with other practices and beliefs "new" to participants.

A prime example of the type of religious message used as an attempt to control a participant's behavior is the way in which Kate was consistently told by the leadership at her fundamentalist Christian university that the problems in her life—however large or small—were due to being rebellious and unsubmissive. She explains the impact these messages had on her in the period of time leading to her suicide attempt during her senior year at the university:

> But I think, really being at [the university] really had a huge influence on that time period in my life. And . . . they gave labels to me like—they didn't . . . I was struggling with my sexuality—but like they always, most of like the people in leadership their were like, said that I was rebellious, that I didn't know how to submit to authority when, in all honesty, I was just trying to figure things out, trying to ask questions. But that was kind of frowned on . . . And I didn't feel like I was in rebellion to God. So it was really confusing to me trying to figure out what was going on and trying things and it wasn't working. And so I guess all those labels and everything they gave me kind of, I think um, I guess I sort of accepted that with all the negative labels that were given to me, I guess I sort of just lumped it all together as well. Just saying, okay, well here's another problem. I'm rebellious, maybe this is why this is happening. Maybe this is why I'm having these thoughts because, you know, I'm not submitting to my authority here at [the university]. Maybe that's why, you know, I'm not sexually attracted to guys. I don't know, you just kind of go through all these things.

Burkitt proves helpful in understanding the effects that these constitutive and interpellative messages have on one's ability to develop one's own voice and perspective—theological or otherwise—amid these strong, denigrating narratives. He argues, "We must not underestimate . . . how difficult it is to find our own voice amidst the voices of others and their ethical evaluations. The fact that we are subject to competing voices and evaluations, and aware of how society in general—the 'generalized other'—might view us, means that our own voices are often internally divided, creating tensions in our relations to others."[7] These tensions amid competing voices are palpable in Kate's sense of being stuck between her desires to "figure out what was going on" and the consistent message that her problems stemmed from her rebellion against God and the authorities of the university.

When the competing voices speak with a religious authority that the individual, to some degree, acknowledges as valid, the difficulty of employing one's own voice of ethical challenge amid internal division and tension is intensified. In some cases, these voices serve to set life within a presumed ultimate context by positing connection to a particular understanding of God. Indeed, what Kate experienced as more damaging to her sense of self-in-relation to God were the ways in which she subtly projected these messages of religious authority figures onto the Divine. She explains, "And that's why I started thinking God thought that way about me. Because all these authorities in my life and people around me, that's what it seemed that they thought. And that was what I was hearing, so I was assuming, if that's what everyone thinks that must be what God thinks."

Hearkening back to a prominent theme from chapter 3, Silas describes the theological doublespeak involved in her interpellation as theologically transgressive. She describes her experience of being labeled "disorderly" within ecclesial contexts this way:

> They say, "Oh, you know, we love you. We care for you from afar, from a distance." But, you know, "No, you're wrong. We can't be around you." The favorite thing of the Christian is cherry picking, "Oh, we have to separate ourselves from those people who walk disorderly. You're just clearly disorderly." Like, okay, I'm disorderly. Thank you. I'm disorderly. Like my friend . . . gave me a button onetime. I was sick in the hospital and it said, "Out of order." That was my button. Not only out of order, disorderly, and we're not going to be around you and we're not going to associate with you. You know, that one whole segment of meaningful people. But then, it's not their fault. It's mine.

Silas contacted me after our interview to describe how our conversation affected her moving forward in her life. Silas *specifically* named the part of our conversation that centered on the brief segment of our interview during which Silas articulated a sense of identity as "disobedient" against "religious rejection." Silas said, "After the interview, and during the interview, things became more clear to me than they had been all these years. That concept of 'civil disobedience against religious rejection' was a big thing to articulate, let alone grasp. So thank you for that." While the experience of rejection because of her "disorderly" conduct is a source of great pain for Silas, it has also become a part of Silas's practice of resistance—a strategy of holding one's own.

In the interview, Silas stated, "I don't want to offend people, but I figure I'm offending people anyway just by being gay, so I might as well mix it up and try to be an activist for human rights while I'm at it." Decades removed from the experience of religious rejection and suicide attempt, Silas is—even now—coming to claim the label of "disorderly" as indicative of a sense of call toward becoming actively disobedient against the religious rejection that affected Silas's own life so profoundly.

The theme of contributing to the wellbeing of others, explored above, continued to shape the way participants lived into their transgressive identity labels in resistance to LGBTQ religious rejection and soul violence. As is quite common for many LGBTQ people in religious contexts, being labeled a "bad influence" on others is part of the justification for removal from the life of the community. Louise illuminated the way this theme came to impact her own life, not because of her own sense of sexual identify, but because of her defiance in the face of the religious rejection of another queer person in her church youth group:

> My friend and I both got kicked out of youth group. He came out and—not to the church, but the kids found out I guess—and so they told on him. And the pastor told him, "I really don't want to have to do this but I think it's a bad influence for the others for you to be here." And I stood up for him so I got kicked out. I didn't come out, but . . . Well, I kind of probably got a little, it got a little heated. Mostly with other youth that were there, not with the pastor. He was like, you know, "It's better if you don't come back," basically. Like to the church and all. And he, what was so painful and this is part of why this really interests me—this is why I was like, not only for myself but I know many people who have experienced the same thing. And he was in a household that, his mom was an alcoholic and his dad was incredibly abusive, and so his escape was youth group and going to the church. And he was very involved but he was also flamboyantly gay. And he attempted suicide the next day after that day. And still, even then, the mom took him to the church and said, "He won't talk to me, maybe he'll talk to you." Because he had been going to that church for years. And even then they weren't supportive. They were like, "Pray more." That was basically their response, just, "Well you just need to pray. You just need to talk to God."

When I asked what they told Louise when they kicked her out of the church, she explained, "They just said that we were causing trouble, basically. I also got kicked out of Sunday school when I was a kid, but that was because I was arguing with the teacher about Adam and Eve."

Further developing the theme of transgressive religious identities working toward the wellbeing of others, Florence described her own transgressive religious practice during her teenage years. Despite her parent's explicit forbidding, Florence secretly volunteered at an inner-city AIDS hospice for a high school community service placement. At this point, Florence was not "out" to others and was only beginning to come to her own self-understanding as a woman attracted to other women. She explains this action in relation to her abovementioned religious conviction that "if the world is not the way that it is supposed to be then part of our job as Christians is to make it the way it is supposed to be." She says,

> I was really compelled by the AIDS crisis and really wanted to volun-
> teer in an AIDS hospice in [my city] . . . So at my school we had to do
> community service as a part of service learning kind of stuff and I
> proposed that as what I wanted to do for my community service and
> my parents wouldn't let me because they said that I would be, it would
> be too much time spent with people who were living a sinful lifestyle
> and that this is the reason why they were suffering from AIDS. So I
> actually disobeyed my parents and went and volunteered there any-
> way secretly.

In addition to acting against the authority of one's parents or the
religious leaders of one's faith community, several participants described
the more overarching impact that living into these "transgressive" labels
had upon the entirety of their theological frameworks. Like Louise above,
who was kicked out of Sunday school for questioning the veracity of the
creation account, and Florence, whose vocational trajectory is profoundly
shaped by a continued resistance to theological heteronormativity, Juliana described the way her questions surrounding her sexual self-understanding and faith tradition affected the totality of her religious practice.
She said,

> Alongside of the gay thing was really just what is this kind of Chris-
> tianity that I'm in, in general? You know, the gay thing became an easy
> target but the real crisis came from the questioning of Christianity. And
> people ask me, "So what was it like being there [at the university] and
> why did you go there? . . . Well, you're so different now it seems like
> couldn't even be, you know, a totally and completely different person."
> I say, "No, I'm the same person. The exact same person." But what
> happened was, I think what happens with any crisis of faith, you end
> up questioning and reach a point where you say, okay I'm starting to
> question things I'm not supposed to question. Am I going to continue
> doing that and see where it takes me? Or am I going to stop? And the
> first two years there were, "No I'm going to. I'm going to cling even
> harder to the belief." . . . So you accept the rhetoric of, you know, the
> insider rhetoric, knowing full well that it's not a fact. That's not the
> truth.

After these first two years at the university, however, Juliana sees "the
gay thing" providing her with the "one really obvious thing that you can
point to that's like the broken cog in a wheel that doesn't allow the wheel
to turn anymore," leading to a far-reaching reappraisal of theological
frameworks and the cultivation of new religious practices. She continued,

> Well, when you have a glaring issue like that that everything you're
> told about it doesn't add up or that you can make it go away or that it's
> a sin or any of these things. And all of those things are under ques-
> tion . . . And you begin to interrogate those questions then the whole
> thing has to crumble. Because you can either keep questioning or not.
> And it came to me, to me it came to an issue of, every time I run, I run

right into this. So I came to the one place where I thought I could be just, you know, that's it. I come here [to the university] and I get my healing and that's it. No, the whole entire framework doesn't work. And so then the whole framework crumbles.

Findlay helpfully points to Patočka's understanding of philosophy, which coincides with the type of questioning of supposed certainties and the simple and clear ways that "knowledge" is unreflectively received and accepted. Findlay says that for Patočka's philosophy, to the extent that this questioning succeeds, "it necessarily challenges the everyday certainties of life; it calls them into question."[8] So rather than a simple "rejection" of religion or belief or spiritual practice, the participants in this research exhibit a profound resubjectivation in the face of subjective precarity. Eribon helpfully describes "resubjectivation" as "the possibility of recreating a personal identity out of an assigned identity. This implies that the acts through which one reinvents one's identity are always dependent on the identity that was imposed by the sexual order. Nothing is created out of nothing, certainly not subjectivities."[9] As an "act of freedom par excellence," Eribon notes that the agential process of resubjectivation "opens the door to the unheard of, the unforeseeable."[10]

Beyond the life-enabling act of resubjectivation and the other-directed acts of care and concern for the wellbeing of others, participants became transgressive *theologians*, reshaping religious belief and spiritual practice in ways that contribute to an understanding of theology's potential to *promote* life and to make life *dangerous*. Queer theologian Marcella Althaus-Reid describes the defiant, rebellious quality of theology that comes into awareness of its conflict with "heterosexual canonical law."[11] In many of the participants, Althaus-Reid's notion of queer theology as is "a theology of loose alliances among sexual dissidents which reconfigures different spaces of thinking and relating to each other"[12] is clearly visible: in the defiance of Thomas in the face of theologies that privilege doctrinal understandings above human lives, in the subversive activity of a young Florence volunteering at an AIDS hospice against her parent's instructions, in Kate's "disobedience" to the religious control of university authorities, and in Louise's standing up to church leaders in defense of her gay peer. In the lives of participants, Althaus-Reid's notions of queer theology takes living form as a "healing theology which dismantles false coherences and ideological scripts in theology in order to allow people to stand up as human beings against a perverse ethics and a perverse theology, which dares to take a departure from monolithic controls concerned with law and not with justice."[13]

Entering the research, I was already influenced by the frameworks of pragmatist theology, viewing theological concepts and categories as human creations of imaginative theological construction. The lives and narratives of participants have further helped me to recognize the importance of actively questioning just what type of world we will construct out of our theological work, religious lives, and spiritual practices. According to Kaufman, the answer to that question must always be "a world within which we can live—fruitfully, meaningfully, creatively, freely."[14]

When what is at stake is the literal livability of one's very life and the fundamental wellbeing of those with whom one is intersubjectively connected, then a radical, queer theological reconstruction must take place, even if that means we become transgressive theologians, an alliance of sexual dissidents, or simply disorderly, disobedient "heretics."

NOTES

1. Michel Foucault, "The Ethics of the Concern of the Self as a Practice of Freedom," in *Ethics: Subjectivity and Truth*, ed. Paul Rabinow, trans. Robert Hurley, et al. (New York: The New Press, 1997), 295.

2. Judith Butler, *Precarious Life: The Powers of Mourning and Violence* (New York: Verso, 2004), xii.

3. Gordon D. Kaufman, *An Essay on Theological Method*, 3rd ed. (Atlanta, GA: Scholars Press, 1995), 38.

4. Kaufman, *An Essay on Theological Method*, 35.

5. Didier Eribon, *Insult and the Making of the Gay Self*, trans. Michael Lucey (Durham, NC: Duke University Press, 2004), 65.

6. Michel Foucault, "Sex, Power, and the Politics of Identity," in *Ethics: Subjectivity and Truth*, ed. Paul Rabinow, trans. Robert Hurley, et al. (New York: The New Press, 1997), 168.

7. Ian Burkitt, *Social Selves: Theories of Self and Society*, 2nd ed. (Los Angeles: SAGE, 2008), 71.

8. Edward F. Findlay, *Caring for the Soul in a Postmodern Age: Politics and Phenomenology in the Though of Jan Patočka* (Albany, NY: State University of New York Press, 2002), 54.

9. Eribon, *Insult and the Making of the Gay Self*, 7.

10. Eribon, *Insult and the Making of the Gay Self*, 7.

11. Marcella Althaus-Reid, "Queer I Stand: Lifting the Skirts of God," in *The Sexual Theologian: Essays on Sex, God and Politics*, eds. Marcella Althaus-Reid and Lisa Isherwood (New York: T&T Clark International, 2004), 100.

12. Althaus-Reid, "Queer I Stand," 106.

13. Althaus-Reid, "Queer I Stand," 108.

14. Kaufman, *An Essay on Theological Method*, 42.

SEVEN

Revisioning the Care of Souls

In the previous chapters, I set the context of the lived human situation that calls for care by illuminating the dynamics of theological narratives perpetuating constitutive violence for many LGBTQ people, setting life on edge and often leading to the attempt of suicide. I examined particular movements that participants made toward life-preserving resistance and the reconstitution of religious practices in the face of this soul violence. These acts of resistance and religious reconstitution are suggestive of the direction of this chapter's constructive contributions to practices of care in relation to LGBTQ lives.

The thesis I put forward at the outset of this study suggests that *foregrounding the metaphor of "soul," holds possibilities for animating the praxis of care in ways that address ethical considerations of the social context in which LGBTQ suicides take place and enhances possibilities for the livability and flourishing of life for LGBTQ persons.* In this chapter, I move in the direction of this thesis by asking: In light of information gleaned regarding the discursive conditions leading to a suicide attempt for participants, what public theological and pastoral care responses are appropriate for addressing the experience of subjective precarity and suicide among LGBTQ persons, promoting possibilities for the livability and flourishing of life? In short, how do the themes developed in the previous two chapters suggest practices in need of development for pastoral theology and pastoral care? Or, what *constructive pastoral theology and praxis* emerges from the data and the theoretical work performed to understand the data?

Gordon Kaufman argues, "The *distinctiveness* of the human over against other forms of life increasingly impressed itself on men and women. As a way of understanding and interpreting this distinctiveness, they developed religious and philosophical conceptions of the *soul*, a distinct nonmaterial kind of reality taken to be the very heart of our human-ness."[1] As I will demonstrate in the brief literature review that follows, the image of "soul" maintains a prime place in the understanding of humanness in the discipline of pastoral care—historically described as the "care of souls." After this review of the "care of souls" tradition, I will deeply engage the interview material alongside my theological and phil-osophical interlocutors in order to future develop—indeed, to *re-vision*—the care of souls tradition for a postmodern era in light of the lived human experience of LGBTQ subjective precarity and suicide experience.

THE "CARE OF SOULS"

I aimed in the previous chapters to address the ways discourses, narra-tives, and stories are operating theologically—setting life within a pre-sumed ultimate context and informing the "deep myths" that constitute an individual's sense of "coreness"—in the lives of LGBTQ persons who come to contemplate and attempt suicide. In this section, I want to illumi-nate a more comprehensive overview of the re-visioned metaphor of "soul" that emerges from the intersections of my research data and my theological and philosophical interlocutors.

Recall Findlay's movement away from a metaphysics and toward an ontology through which the soul can be understood—not as an entity but as the locus of relationship to our own being.[2] Thus, what I aim to do here is not to describe the metaphysical *reality* of soul that is the focus of care, but to illuminate the way a sense of "our relationship to our own being" emerged within the research and points toward the possibility of a descriptive metaphor of "soul" for the praxis of pastoral care. I will do so by foregrounding four themes that I've constructed out of the research toward the practice of care in the context of LGBTQ suicide. I hope that these four themes will ultimately be helpful in understanding how to address the complex relationship between LGBTQ suicide and religion.

The themes are: (1) "enfleshing a storied soul," drawing together the narratival and corporeal aspects of the research; (2) "subjective solidity as a metaphor for 'holding one's own,'" developing an understanding of subjective precarity versus an "ontologically secure" subject position in relation to soul; (3) "narrative unfinalizability as paradoxical precursor to subjective solidity," furthering an understanding of narrative habitus as a critical concept for understanding soul as meaning-making locus; and (4) "collectivist spiritual practice and an intersubjective soul," deindividual-izing the metaphor of soul, further propelling pastoral theology's devel-oping public theological purview.

Enfleshing a Storied Soul

It is evident by now that the literature of narrative therapeutic theory and social constructionism provides a rich framework to my examination of LGBTQ suicide. Given this, however, I take seriously Burkitt's critique of overly textualized metaphors for understanding the human being. He argues, "If what is on offer is the idea of the body as a surface on which a text is written, then the materiality of the productive body slides below the surface of a purely textual analysis where emphasis is placed on the signifying system rather than the lived body."[3] This is certainly a critique that should concern pastoral theologians, as one of the prime historic metaphors guiding the modern practice of pastoral care is Anton Boisen's "living human document"—a textual metaphor for the human *par excellence*. Others in the pastoral literature have, of course, critiqued and revaluated the metaphor of "living human document," perhaps most notably with Bonnie Miller-McLemore's popularization of the "living human web" metaphor, foregrounding the connection of the individual to webs of relationship.[4] This does little, however, to place renewed focus upon the *body*, addressing Burkitt's concern with postmodern textual metaphor usage.

Some pastoral theologians do address the importance of corporeal embodiment in ways that address this critique while still making room for a rich narratival framework to develop. Elaine Graham places the body at the center of moral and social theorizing, reflecting her conviction that the human body serves as the surface upon which the most controversial and pressing dilemmas of the day are made flesh.[5] Furthering the language of "enfleshing," I find the work of Catholic womanist theologian, M. Shawn Copeland, helpful in bringing together a narratival, social constructionist focus with a commitment to taking the corporeal, embodied existence seriously in the praxis of care. Copeland argues, "For the body is no mere object—*already-out-there-now*—with which we are confronted: always the body is with us, inseparable from us, *is* us. But, always, there is a 'more' to you, a 'more' to me: the body mediates that 'more' and makes visible what cannot be seen."[6] It is this "more" that a rich narratival framework helps to uncover, while maintaining that this "more" cannot be entirely distinct from the body as the locus and mediator of the "more."

As explored in chapter 1, Gerkin names the "more" that is mediated and made visible by the body, saying, "Though the individual's cognitive capacities play a significant role, the central core of the self's interpretation of the flow of experience is rooted deeply in the self's affective and imaginative life, the life of symbolism, fantasy, and positive and negative feelings."[7] This points to a view of soul as *rooted* in the flow of experience—particularly, for the purposes of this study, one's bodily and affective experience attached to a person's sense of sexual and gender identity.

Thomas pointed to this in his interview when he described sexuality as that "which is below everything that you know—one of the foundations, the pillars of who you are." Thus, any sense of subjective or ontological "coreness," as Ashbrook names it,[8] connected to the metaphor of "soul" must, of necessity, include the way that the sexual, engendered, enfleshed *body* is a vital part of the sense of coreness that Thomas names as "one of the foundations, the pillars of who you are."

Here, "soul" is a useful metaphor for pointing toward the "more" that is constructed by social discourse, imported into our narrative habitus and enfleshed, inextricably, in the corporeal body and bodily experiences. Suicide is, of course, one such bodily experience through which the "more" of social and theological discourse is enfleshed. In this framework, suicide may be understood as an embodied outcome of what Frank names as a sense of "right and fitting" resolutions toward which an individual's stories should progress—providing a feeling about what move should come next in a narrative progression.[9]

Subjective Solidity as Metaphor for "Holding One's Own"

In chapter 5, I introduced the metaphor of "subjective solidity," drawing on the language of Jan Patočka, as a way of contrasting the subject position of participants who have moved from places of subjective *precarity*—experiencing the unlivability of life and attempts at suicide—to an experience of life's livability. While other metaphors are possible, "solidity" seems to do the conceptual work needed in order to promote the praxis of care in relation to LGBTQ suicide being developed out of this research.

"Solidity," as I am using it as a metaphor for one's sense of "ontological security" in Laing's nomenclature,[10] should not be equated with the solidification of one's narrative habitus, as will become clear in the next section of this chapter. In a more postmodern vein, "solidity" might be better understood as a sense of one's subjective "surefootedness" in life or the capacity for "holding one's own" against damaging and dangerous discourses, thus shedding the modern "ontological" connotations of Laing's phrase. For now, we might understand the experience of "holding one's own" in Frank's words when he argues, "This idiomatic phrase describes situations that begins with a person who has a degree of self-regard; someone with sufficient self-consciousness of what is valuable and worthy of respect about him- or herself."[11] It is clear from the narratives of research participants that this sufficient sense of self-consciousness or value, worth, and respect was considerably diminished leading to what I termed an experience of "subjective precarity" prior to suicide attempt. It is an experience that one participant, Florence, described as an experience of losing all of her anchors in life.

As I moved toward an understanding of how participants dealt with subjective precarity in ways that lead toward the livability of life, I uncovered narratives of participant's theological fortitude and "disorderly" defiance in the face of theological narratives that set life on edge. These were narratives of transgressive theological activity and identity, once foisted and later adopted, toward the livability of life. Here, Findlay is helpful in understanding the relation of this activity in movements toward positions of subjective solidity that I find central to understanding the developing metaphor of "soul." He argues that in the process of movement toward solidity, we not simply reject myth and tradition, but hold to the truths they present to us while refusing to use these myths and traditions as simple answers to life's most difficult problems. Instead, we must face the problematicity of life directly.[12]

This suggests to me the importance of attending to the dialectic of subjective precarity and subjective solidity—the ability of stories to make life dangerous and the abilities of people to "hold their own"—as an important purview for the "care of souls." This focus is congruent with the focus of pastoral theologians upon the "living human web," and maintains the centrality of a narrative, social constructionist philosophical/theological perspective. Our purview is directed toward the ways that audience within the living human web performs legitimizing functions in relation to the subjective precarity/solidity dialectic. Cobb argues, "The legitimizing work is directed to the audience because, indeed, we are legitimate as speakers not through the stories we tell ourselves about ourselves, but through the stories we tell *to others* about ourselves, stories that can then be elaborated by the interlocutors to materialize and anchor the speaker's legitimacy."[13] Among what audiences are our stories about ourselves able to be heard with respect and validation?

Agential movements whereby participants problematized given theological narratives concerning sexual orientation or gender identity, acting in theological defiance as transgressive theologians toward the livability of life, are important clues informing a developing narrative re-visioning of the care of souls. The theological "counternarratives" developed by participants were launched at "the logic, the coherence, and, ultimately, the closure of a dominant narrative, working to upend it."[14] Thus, narrative, pragmatist-informed care of souls must attend to the experiences of subjective precarity and subjective solidity in relation to the factors that inform experience in these two contrasting directions—precarity and solidity—giving particular attention to appreciatively explore the methods persons develop to work with narratives in ways that promote the "holding of one's own."

Narrative Unfinalizability as Paradoxical Precursor to Subjective Solidity

As noted in chapter 5, Didier Eribon speaks to the place of insult in the formation of one's experience of "soul," arguing,

> In insult, it is one's inner sanctum that is threatened, one's heart of hearts, what the spiritual tradition calls the "soul." If a well-targeted insult provokes such a strong echo in the consciousness of the person at whom it is directed, it is because this "soul" has been created through socialization in a world of insult and inferiorization. One could even say that the soul is nothing other than the effect of this socialization. [15]

In my own study of the effects of socialization in relation to LGBTQ suicide, the intensification effect of theological narratives plays an especially important role. "Insult" takes on an even greater power to harm one's sense of "soul" if placed within the context of ultimacy of which theology purports to speak.

For example, theological narratives that purport to represent what is "natural" about the human condition or what is "God's will" in relation to human behavior and relationality all operate to set life within a presumed ultimate context, beyond which no further justificatory appeal may be made. The inferiorization this produces in the lives of some LGBTQ people through theological narratives operating upon the "inner sanctum," or "soul," can lead toward experiences of subjective precarity and the unlivability of life, as demonstrated in chapter 4.

The praxis of the care of souls, informed by narrative frameworks, holds the potential to helpfully address the precarity-inducing narratives that purport to set life within an ultimate context by attending to the ways that persons in need of care may be aided in the proliferation of life-preserving counternarratives. Elaine Graham names the important postmodern corrective to much modern thought and theology by attending to the proliferation of people's own stories, releasing them from imposed ideological and theological frameworks. [16] Attending to and facilitating this narratival proliferation is an especially central function for the care of souls in my developing framework due to the fact that, as Cobb argues, narrative closure (or "foreclosure," in Frank's nomenclature) functions as a form of *violence*. [17] Cobb continues,

> Although all narratives function to close off alternatives to themselves via the process of narrative closure, hard-line narratives contain an injunction against recontextualization and a mandate for compliance. Interlocutors cannot alter the narrative by incorporating new information (characters, episodes, or values) because recontextualization is dangerous, it risks the relationship with the speaker—any move other than the adoption of the hard-line narrative positions an interlocutor as "enemy." Additionally, the hard-line narrative demands compliance through its performance. [18]

I noted previously that the tendency for resistance to what Cobb terms "hard-line narratives" on the part of participants was often met by persons in religious authority labeling participants as disobedient, disorderly, and otherwise transgressive in their religious and spiritual lives (similar to the "enemy" positionality described in Cobb's paragraph above). Through these actions of "disobedience" to religious authority and by becoming transgressive theologians toward the livability of life, participants addressed what Eribon points to as "the products of the subjected soul, inferiorized and conscious of its inferiorization" through the "reinvention" and "refashioning" of the soul[19] that takes place through the proliferation of counternarratives in resistance to narrative foreclosure.

The sense of precarity is met with resistance, aiding a move into a position of subjective "solidity," through a process of living questioningly and provoking problematicity. Many seem to achieve this sense of subjective solidity through the *destabilization* of these "hard-line," theologically intensified narratives that purport to be foundationally, metaphysically secure. Movements into solidity for most participants involved an embrace of the "fundamentally problematic" nature of life in the world whereby the given and seemingly closed narratives were ruptured through processes of questioning, and practices of narrative proliferation were cultivated. The praxis of the care for souls in a narratival vein necessarily helps people to pursue this type of resistance to the violence of narrative foreclosure and move toward the livability of life as it "exists for us as an inherent possibility, one available only if we pursue it."[20]

As Findaly argues, "Caring for the soul occurs via movement that reveals to us our possibilities, and thereby lays a foundation for our choices, our actions."[21] He continues by explaining Patočka's thought, stating,

> [Patočka] argues that in place of metaphysical certainty there is a human consistency, grounded in the way in which we live and the way in which we interrogate reality. Rejecting metaphysical certainty is a vital act, for it appears to leave us defenseless and insecure, while in fact it offers us a unity and a security of a different, particularly human form.[22]

It is this paradoxical defenselessness and insecurity in the face of strong discourses that operate violently against the soul coupled with the willingness and fortitude to level a theological interrogation and critique against presumed "realities" that characterizes the position of subjective "solidity" I witnessed in the lives of participants.

Far from achieving a sense of absolute security by facing the problematic theological narratives, force-with-force, through the theologically *certain* counternarratives, it is the willingness to "project into the past, the future, into imagination, into possibility . . . project[ing] into possibility beyond the limitations of the given"[23] that allowed participants to address the pain and precarity they had experienced. Lives lived in defiance of theological narratives that operate violently upon the soul and diminish life's livability, reveal, as Findlay suggests, that human life is fundamentally problematic.[24] Thus, the movement made by many participants was a movement in the direction of less metaphysically secure, theologically foundational counternarratives and, rather, toward theological and spiritual narratives and practices that value problematicity and living questioningly into the precarity of life.

Embracing the problematic, living questioningly with a commitment to narrative unfinalizability helps to further an understanding of narrative habitus as a critical concept for understanding soul as meaning-making locus, as Gerkin previously imaged "soul" in the pastoral theological literature. Taking Gerkin's thought in a narratival direction, it is helpful to see narratives, along with Frank, as "the resources from which people construct the stories they tell and the intelligibility of stories they hear."[25] The care of souls is, therefore, distinct from other forms of care and counseling in its careful ways of attending to the ways *theological* narratives set life within a presumed ultimate context and profoundly influence the stories people construct and the intelligibility of the stories they hear.

Recall in chapter 1 my exploration of Frank's concept of narrative habitus, foregrounding questions concerning "why certain interpellations have force" and "why . . . people take up the identities they are called to assume."[26] Frank explains a narrative habitus is "the collection of stories in which life is formed and that continue to shape lives."[27] One's narrative habitus disposes one to listen to some stories more attentively than others, repeating some stories more frequently than others.[28] *Theological* narratives make an especially potent claim upon the identities people are called to assume, intensifying the interpellation process by which we take narratives from the collective library into our inner libraries. Consequently, theological narratives hold especially potent power to contribute to the constitutive violence often resulting from these sources by setting these narratives on a transcendent horizon. Freeman illuminated the importance of this horizon of meaning, saying,

> One might therefore speak, cautiously, of the *transcendent horizon* of the life story, by which I refer to those dimensions of the life story that are, finally, about the state and destiny of one's very soul . . . [that] appear to refer to ideals that transcend societal norms and expectations and point toward images of fulfillment and completion that are difficult to contain within a purely immanent framework . . . [providing] a horizon of ultimate meaning and value that conditions the very judgments that can be made about right and wrong, good and bad.[29]

Thus, soul may serve as a helpful metaphorical way to reinvigorate the metaphorical potential to address to the meaning-making capacity of human beings. The term "soul" is able to conceptually take into account the effects of the "transcendent horizon" and theologically laden narratives that construct this narrative habitus, understood as "the dynamic principle by which stories have their effects."[30] In the praxis of care, further treated below, this focus becomes immensely important as narrative habitus predisposes individuals to a sense of "right and fitting" resolutions toward which stories should progress—providing a feeling about what move should come next in a narrative progression.[31] Attending critically to these "next narrative moves" are central to the praxis of care in the context of LGBTQ lives, as experiences of subjective precarity so often lead toward the move of suicide.

Collectivist Spiritual Practice and an Intersubjective Soul

While the transcendent horizon—the theologically laden narratives that purport to set life within an ultimate context—may lead to the unlivability of life and attempts at suicide, participants often enacted resistance to these life-diminishing narratives by replacing, or at very least augmenting, the divine-human transcendence of damaging theological narratives with a human-to-human transcendence. Through this refashioning of religious and spiritual narratives toward a collectivist and altruistic understanding, participants replaced the *telos* of spiritual practices to account not only for the connection between an individual and the individual's sense of the Divine, but also—and perhaps *primarily*—the individual's connection to *others* and contribution to their wellbeing.

As it informs the praxis of care, the theme of intersubjective transcendence also relates to the "enfleshing of the storied soul" treated above. As Shawn Copeland argues, "In and through embodiment, we human persons grasp and realize our essential freedom through engagement and communion with other embodied selves."[32] Similarly, Findlay points to Patočka's work on the relation to the self, saying,

> In order to actualize that self-relation, Patočka writes, our personal being "must go round about through another being. We relate to ourselves by relating to the other, to more and more things and ultimately to the universe as such, so locating ourselves in the world." . . . We become aware of our possibilities not as we delve deeper into ourselves, but as we become involved in other things, as we interact with other beings . . . Our being is, as Patočka notes, a "shared being."[33]

While the theme of collectivist spiritual practices and the refashioning of religion in relation to an self-to-other transcendence occurred again and again throughout my participant interviews, nowhere is the theme of a "shared being," or intersubjective soul, more poignantly represented than in these words from Louise:

I feel like we have to have some sort of invisible connection to one another and to just everything—to the universe, to everything. And in that sense I kind of believe in that, if you want to call that a soul, then yeah, guess I do, I do believe in that. I don't think, I guess you could say it affected my suicide attempt in the sense that at that time, both times, I didn't believe in a soul at all and I didn't believe there was any connection at all. And, so, I think if I had—if I had felt more connected I think that I probably wouldn't have gotten that deep into the rabbit hole. I would have been able to connect. And when you're going through that kind of thing, or when I was going through that kind of thing, it's just like impossible to think that anybody could possibly understand. Or, like, nobody could ever be in your brain, right? Nobody. So therefore, nobody can connect with you because you can't articulate anything. Like, words are so limiting. And then I realized, like, that's bullshit. We're all people. And that was when I kind of like came to terms with the whole oneness thing and, or soul.

For Louise, coming to acknowledge her connection to others—especially in the experience of pain—aided her in the aftermath of her suicide attempt to reach a place of greater subjective solidity. Similarly, in the aftermath of his suicide attempt, Thomas iterated a commitment to defy any theological propositions and understandings that diminished the lives of others. In concrete practice, Florence disobeyed her own parents in relation to theological convictions about the sinfulness of AIDS patients in order to serve dying men in an AIDS hospice in her city, an episode of intersubjective care that she reflects upon today as illustrative of her sense of Christian identity.

These narratives point toward an understanding of soul as an intersubjective "locus of our relationship to our own being"[34] whereby the long conceived "inner sanctum," as Eribon names it above, is hardly *inner* at all. Instead, soul becomes, in Foucault's words, "a reality . . . produced permanently around, on, within the body"[35] in intersubjective relation—bespeaking an experience of transcendence reaching toward the other and produced in relation to the social realm. This intersubjective relation of self-to-other transcendence holds, as many of my participants iterated, an ethical valence. Similarly, Burkitt describes this ethical valance in his work on the social construction of the self, arguing,

In this the self is oriented to the real-life practical tasks of changing or preserving something in the world, including aspects of its own self as part of the social world. The relation to oneself, then, is not "internal" in any sense: when we want to "find" ourselves or change ourselves, we must engage with others in changing aspects of the world through social practice. The self is not separate from its engagement with the world, *but is constituted by the activities it performs.* We make our self as we engage in transforming the material, cultural and interpersonal world.[36]

In many ways, this developing intersubjective ways of conceiving of soul builds upon the pastoral theological treatment of soul by Gerkin who, as noted previously, names the hermeneutical life of the soul as a "profoundly social process," embedding souls in an ecology of meaning and language that is shared with others in historically situated contexts.[37]

This is not a transcendence reaching toward a metaphysical Reality, Divine Being, or transcendent Idea, but a self-to-other, or self-to-world, transcendence that Findlay describes as a movement away from things or objects exerting a hold on us—including, in my estimation, debilitating theological narratives—and *toward* the world as a whole.[38] But this striving toward freedom from the constraints of precarity-inducing theological narratives and the discursive violence they enact upon the soul seems rarely pursued for the benefit of the individual alone. Indeed, nearly every participant in my study emerged from a process of narrival reauthoring with a sense of responsibility for the aid of others in similar positions to their own—an impetus prompting their involvement in this study.

Part of my impetus to reclaim and re-vision "soul" as a vital metaphor for pastoral care is to say that there is more to being human than can be explained and explored by scientific discourse—social scientific or otherwise. Soul is a term with a conceptual history that pushes us to continue a search for non-commodifiable understandings of our humanity—our values, aspirations, and sense of place in the world in relation to others and in relation to an ultimate context. The collectivist understandings and practices developed in the aftermath of suicide attempt, employed in resistance to narratives that operate violently upon the soul, provides a direction we might further pursue in conceiving of how to undertake the praxis of care for souls in a narrival, intersubjective mode.

NOTES

1. Gordon D. Kaufman, *In Face of Mystery: A Constructive Theology* (Cambridge: Harvard University Press, 1993), 107.

2. Edward F. Findlay, *Caring for the Soul in a Postmodern Age: Politics and Phenomenology in the Though of Jan Patočka* (Albany, NY: State University of New York Press, 2002), 63.

3. Ian Burkitt, *Bodies of Thought: Embodiment, Identity & Modernity* (Thousand Oaks, CA: SAGE, 1999), 91.

4. Bonnie J. Miller-McLemore, "The Living Human Web: Pastoral Theology at the Turn of the Century," in *Through the Eyes of Women: Insights for Pastoral Care*, ed. Jeanne Stevenson Moessner (Minneapolis: Fortress Press, 1996), 16.

5. Elaine Graham, *Words Made Flesh: Writings in Pastoral and Practical Theology* (London: SCM Press, 2009), 116.

6. M. Shawn Copeland, *Enfleshing Freedom: Body, Race, and Being* (Minneapolis: Fortress, 2010), 7.

7. Charles V. Gerkin, *The Living Human Document: Re-Visioning Pastoral Counseling in a Hermeneutical Mode* (Nashville: Abingdon, 1984), 101–2.

8. James B. Ashbrook, "Soul: Its Meaning and Its Making," *Journal of Pastoral Care* 45, no. 2 (1991): 160.

9. Arthur W. Frank, *Letting Stories Breathe: A Socio-Narratology* (Chicago: University of Chicago, 2010), 54.

10. R.D. Laing, *The Divided Self: An Existential Study in Sanity and Madness* (Harmondsworth, UK: Penguin, 1960), 42.

11. Frank, *Letting Stories Breathe*, 77.

12. Findlay, *Caring for the Soul in a Postmodern Age*, 106.

13. Sara Cobb, *Speaking of Violence: The Politics and Poetics of Narrative in Conflict Resolution* (New York: Oxford, 2013), 65. Emphasis in original.

14. Cobb, *Speaking of Violence*, 87.

15. Didier Eribon, *Insult and the Making of the Gay Self*, trans. Michael Lucey (Durham, NC: Duke University Press, 2004), 66.

16. Graham, *Words Made Flesh*, 119.

17. Cobb, *Speaking of Violence*, 82.

18. Cobb, *Speaking of Violence*, 82.

19. Eribon, *Insult and the Making of the Gay Self*, 67.

20. Findlay, *Caring for the Soul in a Postmodern Age*, 63.

21. Findlay, *Caring for the Soul in a Postmodern Age*, 65.

22. Findlay, *Caring for the Soul in a Postmodern Age*, 81.

23. Findlay, *Caring for the Soul in a Postmodern Age*, 27.

24. Findlay, *Caring for the Soul in a Postmodern Age*, 61.

25. Frank, *Letting Stories Breathe*, 14.

26. Frank, *Letting Stories Breathe*, 49

27. Frank, *Letting Stories Breathe*, 49

28. Frank, *Letting Stories Breathe*, 53.

29. Freeman, *Hindsight*, 94.

30. Frank, *Letting Stories Breathe*, 54.

31. Frank, *Letting Stories Breathe*, 54.

32. Copeland, *Enfleshing Freedom*, 8

33. Findlay, *Caring for the Soul in a Postmodern Age*, 40–41. Here, Findlay is quoting Jan Patočka, *Body, Community, Language, World*, trans. Erazim Kohák (Chicago: Open Court, 1998), 49.

34. Findlay, *Caring for the Soul in a Postmodern Age*, 63.

35. Michel Foucault, *Discipline & Punish: The Birth of the Prison*, trans. Alan Sheridan (New York: Vintage Books, 1977), 29.

36. Ian Burkitt, *Social Selves: Theories of Self and Society*, 2nd ed. (Los Angeles: SAGE, 2008), 54–55. Emphasis in original.

37. Gerkin, *The Living Human Document*, 110.

38. Findlay, *Caring for the Soul in a Postmodern Age*, 102.

Conclusion

Constructive Lessons for Practices of Care

My aim from the outset of this book included engagement in constructive theological proposals for pastoral praxis. In this conclusion, I will offer constructive proposals for praxis in relation to public theological and individual care responses for addressing the experience of suicide among LGBTQ persons. These proposals aim to promote possibilities for the livability and flourishing of life and to resist the power of stories that make life go badly, that make life dangerous, and that make life, at times, *unlivable* for LGBTQ people. They are firmly rooted in what I learned from the narratives of the nine individuals who participated in this research and shared with me their own strategies for holding their own against the perpetration of soul violence.

SHIFTING FROM *CAUSAL* TO *CONSTITUTIVE* TERMS

As noted earlier, the vast majority of the literature on LGBTQ suicide exists within the social scientific corpus of scholarship. This body of literature informs the work of psychologists, social workers, psychotherapists, and sociologists in addressing the phenomenon through the language and conceptual frameworks endemic within social scientific disciplines. Both my own critical review of this literature and the insights raised by my interview participants serve as an invitation for practitioners of care and counseling to move beyond the social scientific "risk factor" discourse on LGBTQ suicide and to examine, as Flyvbjerg encourages, "the deeper causes behind a given problem" rather than being content "to describe the symptoms of the problem and how frequently they occur."[1]

Individualized and overly psychologized understandings of LGBTQ suicide lead to similarly individualized and overly psychologized "solutions" and methods of prevention. Both my social constructionist reading of the literature and my interviews with participants in this study level a strong critique of the sufficiency of these strategies. Even when social factors—isolation, rejection, stigma, etc.—are named as risk factors negatively affecting the identity development of LGBTQ persons, this veneer of the social does not necessarily challenge the prevailing individualist anthropology in the social sciences. Taylor convincingly argues that, too often, however tightly the dependence of the individual upon the social is conceived, "it is seen in causal terms, and not as touching our very identity."[2]

As it pertains to the contribution of religious and theological narratives upon the lives of LGBTQ people who contemplate and attempt suicide, this research invites practitioners to consider what practices of care could result from de-psychologized understandings of LGBTQ suicide. I aimed in the previous chapters to broaden understandings of LGBTQ suicide through examining the constitutive nature of religious and spiritual narratives upon the embodied, intersubjective sense of self for LGBTQ people. If practitioners move beyond *causal* terms to *constitutive* ones in understanding the factors that contribute to unlivability of life for LGBTQ persons, what practices of care need to be cultivated in order to address the constitutive "deeper causes behind a given problem," as Flyvbjerg phrases it?

The constitutive functions of theological narratives explored in the previous chapters suggest the necessity that caregiving professionals recognize religious practice as an integral part of many LGBTQ persons' multiply layered sense of identity. The bifurcation of LGBTQ identities and religion is common in popular discourse on the intersection of LGBTQ lives and religious involvement, and even creeps slowly in to the ways religion is imagined to operate within social scientific discourses on religion as a "risk factor" contributing to LGBTQ suicide. This is seen, for example, in the way social scientists hypothesize that "exposure to nonaffirming religious settings would lead to higher internalized homophobia, more depressive symptoms, and less psychological well-being,"[3] without accounting for the ways these religious settings simultaneously contribute holistically to a constitutive sense of self for LGBTQ people. Or, in another example, when psychotherapeutic practitioners consider the "loss" of religious or spiritual identity as another type of "loss" similar to that of losing a loved one that then must be grieved,[4] falling short of a more complex, constructionist understanding of the constitutive nature of religious and theological material on the narrative habitus that cannot simply be "lost" or easily "shed."

Treated as a "risk factor," the aim of practice is often to "reduce" the risk posed by religion by aiding LGBTQ persons in separating from or leaving their religious communities. Alternatively, the aim may be to reduce the "risk" through practices of support or therapy aiming at the "integration" of religious/spiritual identities with one's sexual or gender identity through the substitution of more LGBTQ-affirming theological frameworks. Both of these strategies, while at times helpful, rely upon a too clearly delineated bifurcation of religious and LGBTQ identities. This bifurcation in caregiving in the context of LGBTQ suicide grossly overlooks the complexities of the constitutive violence and subjective precarity involved in the experience of individuals.

A constructionist view of religion and theology embedded within my methodology suggests that there are not two clean and easily discernable divisions of narrative content ("secular" versus "theological/religious"). Instead, the methodology allows for the examination of the complex, interwoven, *constitutive* potential of both LGBTQ identity narratives and religious or spiritual narratives upon the lives of individuals in interpenetrating and overlapping ways. This constitutive, rather than additive, perspective is suggestive of ways that practices of care must be cultivated differently.

For example, "leaving church," as discussed in chapter 4, is not enough of a protective maneuver to diminish the potential constitutive violence of theologically laden discourse. Ambient theological messages continue to circulate in wider society, ever contained in the collective library of narratival sources. These sources cultivate one's narrative habitus in ways that operate beyond the conscious recognition of LGBTQ individuals and professionals who work with them. "Uptake" of these narratives from the collective library into the individual, inner library, forming the narrative habitus, must be resisted in a more complex way than encouragements to "leave church" or attempts at simple theological substitution and integration will allow.

Recall from chapter 3 Thomas shared the way that the damaging narratives he encountered as a child could be reactivated almost like ringing a Pavlovian bell:

> It's tone—the tone of what you say. And it's like a bell that goes off. The first time you hear a bell you know what a bell sounds like. The first time you hear that you're an abomination, you remember that tone . . . You know you've just heard again, "You're an abomination."

The ways that these violent spiritual narratives become a part of the narrative habitus are indicative of the careful work that must be performed to address the power of these narratives to harm in ways that move beyond leaving a particular church or religious group.

Beyond interventions aimed at mitigating religious "risk factors," the primary caregiving response to LGBTQ suicide has been suicide "prevention" strategies. While these strategies of prevention are vitally important for intervention, the discourse of "prevention" is not an all-sufficient response to the phenenomon of LGBTQ suicide more broadly. It fails to address Flyvbjerg's "deeper causes behind a given problem." Prevention discourse presents the two dichotomous options as attempting suicide or, preferably, *not* attempting suicide with practitioners leveraging various techniques and interventions to prevent the attempt of suicide. But when the livability of life is so diminished that suicide becomes a thinkable option and the reasons for this diminishment are understood in relation to the forms of discursive violence explained herein, there must be other options for individual action—both for the individuals affected by this precarity-inducing violence and for the practices of professionals. These actions must aim toward the praxis of resistance to the "deeper causes" and not only at preventing the action of suicide itself.

From my findings, I suggest the development of practices incorporating "critique" as an important factor of care in relation to the constitutive violence and subjective precarity LGBTQ people sometimes experience in relation to religious and spiritual narratives. Butler describes "critique" as "an interrogation of the terms by which life is constrained in order to open up the possibility of different modes of living."[5] Moving beyond the bifurcation of LGBTQ and religious identities, we must shift from helping LGBTQ people simply leave their churches or religious traditions when they become damaging—though, at times, this may still need to occur as well. Instead, we must develop strategies for strengthening individuals' capacity for refashioning religious narratives and spiritual practices through "thinking questioningly" in relation to these narratives.[6] A strategy of care incorporating "critique" recognizes spiritual resources as potential practices for resistance to precarity-inducing discursive violence as exhibited in many of my participants and assists LGBTQ individuals in opening up possibilities for "different modes of living," as Butler suggests.

For some, like Florence and Thomas, this resistance took the shape of refashioning religious practice within the religious traditions in which they were formed—in this case, Protestant Christian—albeit with the shifting of denominational affiliation. For others, like Louise, resistance and the refashioning of religious practice took the form of larger philosophical shifts and the construction of new spiritual practices that are significantly removed from the religious tradition of her upbringing—in her case, Catholicism. Thus, whether one "rejects" or "leaves" one's prior religious tradition, the development of LGBTQ individuals' capacity for "critique" or "thinking questioningly" in relation to religious narratives and theological practices opens "the possibility of different modes of living."[7]

Strategies formed around "critique" take fully into account the *constitutive*, rather than simply *causal*, place that religion and spirituality plays in the lives of many LGBTQ persons leading to the attempt at suicide. Such practices of care must incorporate the critical question of this study regarding how the narratives that purport to position human beings and the world in relation to "God"—or at least the word "God"—form the "deep myths" that are constitutive of a person's *sense* of coreness. And these practices must address how the narratival placement of human lives into a presumed "ultimate context" through theologically laden narratives shapes the liveability of lives, opening the possibilities for both flourishing and subjective precarity.

This shift from dominant social scientific discourse on LGBTQ suicide toward understandings shaped by social constructionism calls for the cultivation of new practices that move beyond the examination of "risk factors" and a sole focus upon prevention strategies. This shift from "causal" terms to "constitutive" understandings of religion's influence in relation to LGBTQ suicide invites practitioners to develop more nuanced understandings of religion, spirituality, and theological discourse and the ways these narratives come to shape a narrative habitus which, in turn, predisposes individuals to a sense of "right and fitting" resolutions toward which stories should progress—providing a feeling about what move should come next in a narrative progression.[8] Without such a nuanced, constitutive perspective on religious and theological influences, it is likely that practices of care will produce unnecessarily bifurcated options for caring praxis and fail to account for the complexity of constitutive factors that make up the core sense of "identity" and meaning-making capacity for LGBTQ persons seeking care.

AGENTIAL NARRATIVAL DECONSTRUCTION

In the last chapter, I suggested that the care of souls should incorporate the themes "enfleshing a storied soul," "subjective solidity as a metaphor for 'holding one's own,'" "narrative unfinalizability as paradoxical precursor to subjective solidity," and "collectivist spiritual practice" bespeaking "an intersubjective soul." Beyond the techniques of deconstructing "problem stories" and strengthening "preferred narratives" common to narrative therapeutic technique, this study is suggestive of narrative techniques of care and counseling that looks critically at narratives that make life precarious. These practices bring into the care and counseling process elements of "critique," in the sense of Butler cited above, and "thinking questioningly," as exhibited by participants.

As early as the mid-1980s, when narrative *therapeutic* theory was still in its infancy and not yet largely impactful on the North American scene,[9] Charles Gerkin argued that humans beings and behavior exhibit a narrative structure, bringing past, present, and future together in acts of interpretation and decision making in every situation. Thus, Gerkin argues, "Praxis—and, most particularly, practical theological thinking in the situation of praxis—always involves an essentially narrative structure."[10] Through the interview materials, I have drawn extensively upon theological frameworks of interpretation offered by pragmatist theologians like Kaufman, Davaney, and others, which seem especially pertinent source to aid in the development of the praxis of practical and pastoral theological engagement with the narrative structure of human situations that call for care.

Kautman says our faith, or "our deepest-lying concerns and commitments," "define our very being—who we are, how we understand ourselves, what our existence is and what it means to us, what we value most highly and are devoted to."[11] As such, he argues that these deep-lying concerns and commitments are not easily subject to our "direct manipulation" and, in fact, come to shape our deliberate actions in ways that sometimes defy conscious intention.

Kaufman continues with a paragraph that is particularly fitting to guide care and counseling in the context of LGBTQ suicide, saying,

> The most we can hope to do with respect to these matters, then, is try to articulate, and thus get clearer to ourselves, these deep-lying pictures and conceptions of life and the world which we take for granted; and then, perhaps—where we find tensions and contradictions and imbalances threatening to render us impotent or to pull us apart—attempt to adapt or fit these to one another in such a way that they can begin (in due course) to grow together, mutually fructifying and reinforcing one another, as they mature into a better integrated, more holistic faith.[12]

Adopting a pragmatist theological perspective that theology "is, and always has been," an act of "imaginative construction,"[13] I affirm alongside Davaney that theological traditions "embody both life-giving and life-denying possibilities and are ever the conveyors of social and political power."[14] Beyond narrative techniques of deconstructing "problem stories" and strengthening "preferred narratives," narrative techniques of care and counseling that aim to address religious and spiritual narratives that make life precarious must cultivate the capacity of persons to engage in "critique" and "thinking questioningly" in relation to these narratives, thus facilitating the capacity to engage in religious refashioning and "transgressive" theological construction toward the livability of life, as evidenced in the narratives of my participants. But beyond the implications this holds for the practice of care and counseling with individuals, it holds important implications for those involved in cultivating communities of care in contexts like congregations and other religious institutions.

This movement is a direct and self-conscious praxis aimed toward the cultivation of "identities"—caring for the souls of persons as embodied, intersubjective beings seeking to hold their own amid competing and sometimes dangerous narritival sources. As Namsoon Kang argues, "People's participation in the theological discourse can distort or transform their identities and understandings of self, the world, and the Divine."[15] Thus, care and counseling practitioners may see their work at the interrelation of pastoral postures of deconstructive listening and co-critique of theological frameworks that set life on edge *and* attention to the construction of individuals' constitutive sense of identity in relation to narratives that "define our very being—who we are, how we understand ourselves, what our existence is and what it means to us, what we value most highly and are devoted to."[16]

The general contours of a caregiving role emerging from this critique and constructive proposal take shape around the facilitation of processes of deconstructive conversation on an interpersonal level, and deconstructive, collaborative theological praxis on a broader level. This deconstructive praxis, attending to the ways that narratives that operate to set life within a presume ultimate context, look critically at how narratives "embody both life-giving and life-denying possibilities and are ever the conveyors of social and political power."[17] More than a shift in *role* for the caregiver, the constructive critique I am developing suggests a change in *posture* for the caregiver in relation to LGBTQ lives.

Any shifts in practices of care that develop from this posture are aimed more clearly and explicitly toward the praxis of strengthening and supporting the agential capacity of persons to engage in imaginative theological construction with the potential for developing Althaus-Reid's notion of "a theology of loose alliances among sexual dissidents which reconfigures different spaces of thinking and relating to each other."[18] Here again, Kaufman is helpful in exploring the place of agential capacity in theological construction, arguing,

> Agency is not a static condition that simply is what it is: agency is, rather, a living process, a *creative* process continuously engaged as much in transformation of itself—of opening one's self to new and different possibilities of action—as in transformation of external realities. By virtue of this power of acting upon ourselves, we are able to take responsibility not only for our particular choices and actions but—in certain respects—for our very selfhood, for what we have become and what we shall become.[19]

I witnessed this agential reconfiguration of relation to self and other and deconstruction of identity narratives in relation to religious and theological narratives in the stories of my participants who took on an attitude of defiance and theological fortitude in the face of damaging narratives that served to set life on edge. Caregiving practitioners willing to allow these witnessed examples to guide the praxis of care in relation to LGBTQ suicide can be assisted by asking two key questions Frank offers for narrative-oriented practitioners: "What other narrative resources, if available, might lead to different stories and change people's sense of possibility in such settings?" And, "What might be preventing those alternative narrative resources from being mobilized?"[20] Similar to the goal of dialogical narrative analysis, the praxis of care in relation to agential deconstruction of theological and identity narratives is in "assisting people to become more reflective narrators of their lives."[21]

The test for the efficacy of these narrative and pragmatist-informed practices of care must be a pragmatist one. Kaufman argues that theological "categories and concepts have been created in the efforts of men and women to grasp and comprehend their developing experience, and they have meaning only so far as they succeed in forming and interpreting experience."[22] Thus we must ask of our practices of care: "What forms of human life do these conceptions of its context facilitate? Which forms inhibit? What possibilities do they open up for men and women? Which do they close off?"[23]

This pragmatist theological test became evident in the narratives rendered by my interview participants. For example, as Louise explained regarding the profound theological and philosophical shifts from her Catholic background to her current perspectives on spirituality, "Whether it be true or not, it's just a choice. It's almost like I've chosen to believe that because that's what I find comforting." More than comforting, however, these deconstructed and refashioned religious and spiritual narratives actively aid Louise in the livability of her own life.

Similarly, Juliana rejects her own need for embracing affirming Christian theologies in relation to LGBTQ people as unnecessary in the development of her spiritual and religious identity. She did, however, state, "I used to have a very strong reaction to that whole thing and now it's kind of like, with my mom, if that's what works, well good. Good. Glad you found that." The test of affirming theology's usefulness for Juliana is in the narrative's ability to "work" toward the livability of life for others.

Thomas, too, exhibited a strong pragmatist bent in his desire to defend others from "understandings" that stand in the way of love and embrace into community. He explained the pragmatist criteria for judging the suitability of theological narratives, saying, "The message of Christ is hope, love, unconditional. Done. Anything that implies anything different—the feeling of it, an understanding that messes with it—anything at all, just get your shit straight. That's wrong."

Beyond the development of practices of welcome and LGBTQ-affirming theologies, these findings call caregiving practitioners and religious communities toward truly transgressive, queer theological practices that hold pragmatist theological criteria for the usefulness of narratives that set life within a presumed ultimate context. Simple theological substitution of condemnatory theologies for affirming ones, while perhaps helpful in some circumstances, falls short of strengthening the *agential capacity* of individuals and communities for narratival deconstruction and religious reconfiguration and refashioning toward the livability of life. Recall Kaufman's claim that agency "is not a static condition that simply is what it is: agency is, rather, a living process, a *creative* process continuously engaged as much in transformation of itself—of opening one's self to new and different possibilities of action—as in transformation of external realities."[24]

Pastoral practices developed with the aim of facilitating and strengthening the capacity for agential narratival deconstruction must give careful attention to ruptures "when our faith in the world is shaken that we are forced to abandon objective, simply given conceptions of meaning." As Findlay argues, we move away from the taken-for-granted tentative fact and return to it with a greater degree of awareness and meaning.[25] The shattering experiences of life experienced by my interview participants at the convergence of LGBTQ identities and theological narratives that set life within a presumed ultimate context led to reconstructive acts of "new" religious meanings and spiritual practices that afforded the subjective solidity needed in order to experience livability.

But, as Findlay warns and my participants exhibited, there is no end to problematicity in our search for and initiation of meaning.[26] Instead, the movement made by many of my participants was a movement toward narrative unfinalizability in the direction of less metaphysically secure, theologically foundational counternarratives and, rather, toward theological and spiritual narratives and practices that *valued* problematicity and living questioningly amid the precarity of life.

Perhaps most importantly, caregiving practitioners and religious communities cannot simply respond to the circumstances described in the past three chapters out of *their own* imagination for what might be helpful in the lives of LGBTQ people—even when these imaginings are in the direction of LGBTQ affirmation. Additionally, the prevailing social scientific perspectives on LGBTQ suicide can take us only so far in practices of prevention and risk reduction. Instead, caregiving practitioners and religious communities must actively hear the voices of LGBTQ people as creative, agential and, at times, transgressive theologians toward the livability of life with the capacity and ability to open our *institutional practices* and *communities* "to new and different possibilities of action—as in transformation of external realities."[27]

Caring praxis that enhances the livability of life cannot be characterized or categorized with any finality. But an initial descriptor of how we might recognize we are on our way toward such a praxis-in-the-making, toward transformative ends that enhance the livability of life, begins with the practice of rupture. Namely, such caregiving practices look for possibilities to rupture the coherence of a narrative that is operating violently to diminish the lives of persons or groups. As Cobb argues, "The coherence of the narrative contributes to its closure . . . stabilized such that these events cannot be destabilized or altered."[28] She further posits that narrative closure functions as a form of violence, where as "an injunction against recontextualization and a mandate for compliance" resist the incorporation of new, counter, or subjugated narrative material.[29]

In order to move toward a constructive theology of *possibility*, a theory of what might *become*, a type of *praxis-in-the-making*, caregivers must develop facility working at the points of rupture within theologically secure, metaphysically well-grounded narratives in order to invite movement toward liminal spaces of subjunctive possibility. In these spaces,

Cobb contends, the possibility for "narrative transformation" is possible, allowing people to "unhook from their roles and the markers associated with those roles."[30] This pastoral activity becomes especially pertinent when these roles and their narratival next-moves become marked by narratives of ultimacy that induce a sense of precarity, foreclosing upon movement toward the livability of life.

CARE OF SOULS AS POLITICAL PRAXIS: PUBLIC THEOLOGICAL AND ETHICAL RESPONSES TO LGBTQ SUICIDE

Form a Foucouldian perspective, studying LGBTQ suicide may be considered a way of studying "power" at the point at which it becomes "capillary."[31] This means, of course, not simply investigating the ways religious narratives create factors of "risk" for LGBTQ persons—which seems the prime concern of many social scientists in relation to LGBTQ suicide. Instead, investigating power at its capillary points implies an investigation into struggles against certain forms of subjection and subjectification through the constitutive effects of dominant discourse—in this case, religious, spiritual, and theological narratives. A focus upon the power of discourse at the points at which it becomes capillary draws a pastoral theological focus upon LGBTQ suicide into a public theological realm where subjectification is addressed more broadly than on an individual basis. This invites a re-visioning of the once highly individualized metaphor, "care of souls," as *political praxis* and furthers pastoral theological engagement with public theological projects.

Stephen Pattison argues, "If theology is worth thinking about at all then it should be of public interest well beyond the religious community."[32] Contrary to a public theological purview *negating* a focus upon the "soul" as a metaphor for the locus of care, philosophers like Patočka, Foucault, and Kwame Anthony Appiah[33] turned their attention *toward* the "soul" as an integral part of their work on the "public" and the "political." A public theological focus upon the phenomenon of suicide among LGBTQ persons foregrounding the metaphor of soul as I have developed it here must take seriously Kang's admonition that "we should recognize the significance of theological discourse as public discourse that affects the lives of people in a concrete way."[34] The understandings of LGBTQ suicide and religious and spiritual narratives that I have developed through the tools of socionarratology, dialogical narrative analysis, and pragmatist theological perspectives provide critical source material for better addressing the way that public discourse affects the lives of people in concrete ways—setting life within presumed ultimate contexts and, at times, setting life on edge.

Cover, too, is critical of the overly individualized models of response that I have pointed to again and again throughout this study, but he goes further to critique social change models aimed to address prejudi ⅃ attitudes and discrimination against LGBTQ persons as the focal point of LGBTQ distress leading to suicidal ideation and action. Cover points us toward a more robust form of ethical response to LGBTQ suicide, arguing,

> An ethical response, however, is more than simply developing interventionist policies, expanding counselling or engaging in social change such that queerness seems less shameful or less normal, more tolerated or more included. Rather, the nature of an ethical response is, by necessity, complex yet can lead to understanding how different responses—both pragmatic and philosophic—need to be developed outside of the normative frameworks through which queer youth suicide has generally become a policy, social or research issue.[35]

Cover helpfully suggests that a complex ethical response must look beyond the normative framework typically employed at all levels of LGBTQ suicide prevention, guided primarily by the discourse of psy-experts.

Erwin names two of the normative, operative assumptions in these psychologically informed social change models addressing the reality of heterosexism. First, if one holds heterosexism as the cause of mental distress among LGBTQ persons, then heterosexism "must be actively addressed through efforts to change the laws, institutions, and attitudes that oppress."[36] Second, the mental distress caused by heterosexism—feelings of isolation, shame, stigmatization, etc.—must be addressed through individual, group, or family counseling which takes into account the environmental causes of distress alongside other sources of psychological distress not related to one's sexuality.

While changing stigmatizing laws, institutional norms, and personal attitudes are of continued and vital importance, these strategies of social change fail to fully address the call Cover issues for social change strategies that "need to be developed outside of the normative frameworks."[37] While some participants, like Silas, named the changing legal landscape as an encouraging factor in their lives, my findings from participant narratives adds further critique to an overdependence upon the language and frameworks of psy-experts to understand what is useful or helpful about this strategy of social support and grassroots activism. Rather than simply alleviating "mental distress" caused by shaming and stigmatizing environments, participants revealed other ways that addressing the points at which power becomes capillary in the process of subjectification becomes central to the care of souls. Participants foregrounded stories exhibiting agential capacity to challenge and change dominant narratives and the importance of performing this activity with the wellbeing of others explicitly in view.

ι   ʰologist Thomas Joiner, a leading suicidologist, argues that a lack of a sense of belongingness is a key factor in suicide ideation and completion.[38] While this lack of a sense of belongingness operates on an interpersonal level, my research suggests that it is also related to a sense of "belongingness" to the sociocultural and religious discursive space. Indeed, Oliver argues that it is impossible to gain a sense of belonging to the community with a lack of participation in or belonging to the meanings of dominant culture or the social space to create meaning for oneself.[39] Burkitt furthers this social constructionist understanding of persons arguing that our relation to our "self" is not actually "internal" as it is so often imaged in psychological discourse. Instead, he argues, "When we want to 'find' ourselves or change ourselves, we must engage with others in changing aspects of the world through social practice."[40] The self, in this perspective—congruent with the findings in my research with participants—"*is constituted by the activities it performs.*"[41]

Thus, this agential activity whereby participants engaged in narrative deconstruction and religious reconfiguration and refashioning toward the livability of life is clearly not performed for the psychological benefit of the individual alone. Participants' descriptions of their own processes of agential participation in changing aspects of the world that diminish the livability of life suggest that *caring for others* through these agential theological activities is an important component of *caring for one's own soul*. Indeed, drawing upon Plato, Patočka views care for the soul *requiring* that the act of care be performed in constant reference to shared life in the polis—the *political*—directly connecting, as Findlay argues, "the spiritual life to praxis."[42] He continues,

> Our relation to ourselves, our self-understanding as autonomous entities, is therefore not the sole factor constitutive of our being. Because of our corporeity and the nature of our lives as played out in communities, we relate to other beings, both objects and persons, and we relate to the world that is their context. These relations are part of our being, they enable our successful self-relation.[43]

I believe this care for others through intervention in the sociocultural and religious discursive space is one of the factors to which we might attribute the widespread popularity and participation in the It Get's Better Campaign. While limited in many ways,[44] this campaign opened (cyber)space for LGBTQ people (along with many straight and cisgender contributors) to reach out toward unknown others in the hopes of engaging with them in changing the discourse on the livability of LGBTQ lives by issuing messages of hope for the future to LGBTQ people living in seeming unlivable situations, whether because of school bullying, family rejection, religious shaming, or the isolating pressures of the closet. It is a project allowing LGBTQ people to intervene in discursive, narratival deconstruction and reconstruction—sometimes with explicit theological valance—with the aim of helping other LGBTQ people be better able to hold their own.

I observed this same impetus in the lives of my research participants through which they developed a sense of self-to-other transcendence and engaged in collectivist spiritual practices aimed toward helping others in situations similar in some ways to their own. If the care of souls is re-visioned as political praxis with public theological implications, I believe this impetus toward the care of others as integral to the care of one's own soul is indicative of the type of public theological praxis in need of development. Taking seriously the restorative nature of this care for others exhibited in the narratives of my participants, a public theological praxis must be rooted in the wisdom of lived human experiences of subjective precarity and the praxis of resistance toward subjective solidity and the livability of life. As Sharon Welch convincingly argues,

> The struggle against oppression gains power by drawing on people's heritage and experience, not merely on abstractions from their experience. A concept of freedom is most effective as it is rooted in the imagination of the people to be freed, if it does indeed speak to something in their experience and their history . . . This makes possible the recognition of unique or divergent forms of resistance and freedom. [45]

To a degree, this is descriptive of the academic conversation that is taking place within the literature of queer theology. My experience with participants, however, raises questions for me concerning where this generative conversation is taking place in *non-academic* spaces, ecclesial or otherwise. And, further, where these deconstructive conversations and refashionings of religious practices and transgressive theological thinking toward the livability of life *might* take place if the space was appropriately cultivated. A type of public, collaborative theological project in need of development should foreground Arthur Frank's questions of socionarratology when he asks,

> How might people's lives change if they heard their own stories with enhanced reflective awareness and if they heard others' stories with a more generous sense of what makes these stories viable representations of the lives those storytellers live? . . . Stories are representations not so much of life as it is, but of life as it is imagined, with that imagination shaped by previous stories. Storytelling is a dialogue of imaginations. This dialogue is real in its consequences for how people act. [46]

Just as for Frank, storytelling is a dialogue of imaginations, so too for pragmatist-informed theology performed in collaborative, dialogical engagement with lived human experience is an imaginative endeavor, working and reworking the narratives and symbols that set life within a presumed ultimate context—an "imaginative construction" of "a comprehensive and coherent picture of humanity in a world under God," as Kaufman puts it.[47]

In a more expansive sense intimated by Kaufman, my methodology enlarges the notion, "under God," into a phrase free enough from theologically realist notions to allow for pastoral theological engagement with *a sense of ultimacy* in view, whether explicitly containing terms typically designated as "theological" or not. These narratives and symbols of ultimacy are ones bespeaking "who we are, how we understand ourselves, what our existence is and what it means to us, what we value most highly and are devoted to."[48] What is most important in my inquiry is how persons view their own lives within a presumed ultimate context and how their next narrative moves exist in relation to their individual and intersubjective understandings of this context of ultimacy.

Spaces cultivated through the foregrounding "dialogues of imagination" in theological deconstruction would be public, shared spaces in which participants listened to the stories and narratives of their own and others' lives and religious and spiritual perspectives for what Sharon Welch describes as "strategically important ideas" whereby "the ideas, doctrines, and symbols of the Christian faith are understood in terms of their function in the struggle of people for liberation."[49] My participants, oftentimes largely in *isolation* from supportive dialogical community, agentially engaged in the deconstruction and refashioning of the strategically important theological ideas and spiritual practices which served to aid in their movements from subjective precarity toward the livability of life.

The intentional cultivation of public, shared spaces for collaborative theological engagement where this can take place through a "dialogue of imaginations" moves a pastoral theological and ecclesial engagement with LGBTQ suicide toward Kang's admonition that "Christianity as an institutionalized religion needs to undo and move beyond its history of sin by institutionally repenting and theologically amending its great fallacy and wrongdoing"[50] by encouraging and facilitating people's critical deconstructive engagement with theological narratives and transforming understandings of self, world, and the Divine. Kang's notion of Christianity's "history of sin" include the myriad ways Christian theological discourses have carried forth the oppression of "others"—"women, Jews, Moors, pagans, infidels, and heathens"—through crusades and inquisitions of many kinds, eventuating in violence, destruction, and death for many.[51]

Since much of the violence against myriad "others" is perpetuated and justified through the production of theological discourses offering a "sanctioned rationale for such oppression and exclusion," public theological engagement must be aimed at loci of the production of theological discourse.[52] With a deconstructive gaze, and congruent with pragmatist theological commitments, the "truth" of theological constructions that emerge from such spaces of critical imaginative dialogue "is measured not by their correspondence to something eternal," Welch argues, "but by the fulfillment of its claims in history, by the actual creation of communities of peace, justice, and equality."[53]

The possibilities for this type of public theological praxis are myriad and must always be developed contextually. Just like a "concept of freedom," public theological praxis in support of the livability of life for LGBTQ people "is most effective as it is rooted in the imagination of the people"[54] most affected by the praxis. Thus, a *collaborative theological praxis* emerging from this vision privileges the place of storytelling as "a dialogue of imaginations . . . real in its consequences for how people act."[55] Placing this perspective of stories and narratives in theological context, Kang helpfully argues, "Theological discourse can be, in and of itself, a form of identity and solidarity . . . functionin[g] in various ways as sites of contestation and resistance, of forming new religious and personal identities, and of building solidarities."[56]

Addressing the lack of a sense of belongingness within the context of sociocultural and religious discursive space, public theological praxis might carry on the caregivers' task as explained above as working to rupture the coherence of a narrative that is operating violently to diminish the lives of persons or groups. These points of discursive rupture aim to develop narratival resources "outside of the normative frameworks" that typically emerge into "a policy, social or research issue."[57]

Instead of tinkering with theological pronouncements—even if these discursive moves aim in the direction of increasing affirmation for LGBTQ lives—collaborative theological praxis as a "form of identity and solidarity" encourages the plurivocality and proliferation of theological narratives rooted within lived human experience. Michael Hogue posits that this can only take place when we learn that "no normative perspective exhaustively captures the whole truth of reality," that "multiple perspectives together offer a more adequate interpretation," and that "those vulnerable persons and communities whose lives and well-being are most directly at stake in a given moral situation should be granted a leading role in analyzing and responding to the conditions they face."[58]

At this point, Hogue's words should be descriptive in the reader's mind of what I have been aiming toward throughout the book as a pastoral theological engagement with LGBTQ suicide. A contextual, collaborative theology, however, becomes a *public theology* when it is undertaken in public. That is, as Hogue helpfully clarifies, when "the tasks of critique, clarification, and normative negotiation occurs outside of the religious community proper and in relation to the broader sociocultural conditions, processes, spheres, and political and moral challenges of human life."[59]

As theologians, practitioners of ministry, and religious communities engage in these broad sociocultural challenges affecting the lives of

LGBTQ people, the question must be continually raised: *What narratives on LGBTQ lives are operating with too much finality to the detriment of LGBTQ people?* The most obvious are those narratives portraying the LGBTQ person as "sick," "sinful," or morally "disordered." These narratives are already meeting the challenge of myriad religious communities moving toward LGBTQ-affirming theological stances.

In some sense, however, any public theological activity that transcends what have become the "normative frameworks" for LGBTQ faith-based activism (i.e., activism focusing upon legal equality and ecclesial inclusion and affirmation) are working to rupture discourses that, while aiming toward the increase of justice, hold potential to become debilitating, finalized narratives of LGBTQ wellbeing. These narratives and normative aims, while theologically affirming of LGBTQ person's dignity and worth, must also be critiqued for the ways their coherence is developed around the noramativity of citizenship rights and economic advantages through acquiring inclusion into legal and communal structures upholding certain racial, class, national, and gender privilege.

Public theological activism that addresses broader concerns of queer collectives like LGBTQ youth homelessness, familial rejection, LGBTQ immigration rights—all underrepresented concerns in dominant iterations of faith-based LGBTQ activism—serves to rupture the coherence of narratives that have become normative frameworks for understanding LGBTQ lives. Additionally, public theological demonstrations of *repentance* for churches' complicity in Christianity's "history of sin" in relation to LGBTQ lives could work toward directing the attention of religious communities toward the recognition of "the significance of theological discourse as public discourse that affects the lives of people in a concrete way."[60]

Pragmatist-informed public theological praxis thus illuminates the ways that theology requires continued communal and contextual revision and reconstruction, guided by the voices of those with most at stake in the livability of life in light of these theological perspectives. Because it affects the lives of people in concrete ways, as Kang reminds us, the activity of public theological praxis is not ancillary to the care of souls but is, instead, a vital part of this care.

Toward the end of my interview with Louise, she expressed that the words "everything is going to be fine" just weren't sufficient to help her in the time leading up to her suicide attempt. I asked her what message she *would* have found helpful in that time of precarity. Her words in response are a fitting end to this exploration of the souls of queer folks:

> I guess, "The world is bigger than you think it is and not everybody is
> the same. Think of everything you haven't seen yet and everything you
> haven't done and everything you haven't experienced. Nothing is a

binary, nothing is a dichotomy, and everything is subjective. There'
just unlimited possibilities in life."

NOTES

1. Bent Flyvbjerg, "Five Misunderstandings about Case-Study Research," in *Qualitative Research Practice*, ed. Clive Seale, Giampetro Gobo, Jaber F. Gubrium, and David Silverman (London: Sage, 2007), 395.

2. Charles Taylor, *Human Agency and Language: Philosophical Papers 1* (New York: Cambridge University Press, 1985), 8.

3. David M. Barnes and Ilan H Meyer, "Religious Affiliation, Internalized Homophobia, and Mental Health in Lesbians, Gay Men, and Bisexuals," *American Journal of Orthopsychiatry* 82, no. 4 (2012): 505.

4. Andrew William Wood and Abigail Holland Conley, "Loss of Religious or Spiritual Identity Among the LGBT Population," *Counseling and Values* 59 (2014): 105.

5. Judith Butler, *Undoing Gender* (New York: Routledge, 2004), 4.

6. This suggestion is similar to the deconstructive work incorporated into narrative therapeutic theories, however, that literature has not sufficiently addressed the complexities of deconstructing theologically intensified narratives that purport to set life within an ultimate context. I believe this study lends itself to the further development of these narrative therapeutic deconstructive strategies.

7. Butler, *Undoing Gender*, 4.

8. Arthur W. Frank, *Letting Stories Breathe: A Socio-Narratology* (Chicago: University of Chicago, 2010), 54.

9. I date the beginning of more widespread North American engagement with Narrative Therapy to 1990 with the publication of Michael White and David Epston, *Narrative Means to Therapeutic Ends* (New York: Norton, 1990).

10. Charles V. Gerkin, *Widening the Horizons: Pastoral Responses to a Fragmented Society* (Philadelphia: Westminster, 1986), 52.

11. Gordon D. Kaufman, *In Face of Mystery: A Constructive Theology* (Cambridge: Harvard University Press, 1993), 434.

12. Kaufman, *In Face of Mystery*, 434.

13. Gordon D. Kaufman, *An Essay on Theological Method*, 3rd ed. (Atlanta, GA: Scholars Press, 1995), ix.

14. Sheila Greeve Davaney, *Pragmatic Historicism: A Theology for the Twenty-First Century* (Albany, NY: State University of New York Press, 2000), 84.

15. Namsoon Kang, *Cosmopolitan Theology: Reconstituting Planetary Hospitality, Neighbor-Love, and Solidarity in an Uneven World* (St. Louis: Chalice, 2013), 7.

16. Kaufman, *In Face of Mystery*, 434.

17. Davaney, *Pragmatic Historicism*, 84.

18. Marcella Althaus-Reid, "Queer I Stand: Lifting the Skirts of God," in *The Sexual Theologian: Essays on Sex, God and Politics*, eds. Marcella Althaus-Reid and Lisa Isherwood (New York: T&T Clark International, 2004), 106.

19. Gordon D. Kaufman, *Jesus and Creativity* (Minneapolis: Fortress, 2006), 86.

20. Arthur W. Frank, "Practicing Dialogical Narrative Analysis," in *Varieties of Narrative Analysis*, eds. James Holstein and Jaber F. Gubrium (Thousand Oaks, CA: SAGE, 2012), 44–45.

21. Frank, "Practicing Dialogical Narrative Analysis," 48.

22. Kaufman, *An Essay on Theological Method*, 10.

23. Kaufman, *An Essay on Theological Method*, 38.

24. Kaufman, *Jesus and Creativity*, 86.

25. Edward F. Findlay, *Caring for the Soul in a Postmodern Age: Politics and Phenomenology in the Though of Jan Patočka* (Albany, NY: State University of New York Press, 2002), 167–68.

26. Findlay, *Caring for the Soul in a Postmodern Age*, 178.

2' Kaufman, *Jesus and Creativity*, 86.

2. Cobb, *Speaking of Violence: The Politics and Poetics of Narrative in Conflict Resolu* (New York: Oxford, 2013), 69.

29. Cobb, *Speaking of Violence*, 82.

30. Cobb, *Speaking of Violence*, 104.

31. Michel Foucault, *Society Must Be Defended*, trans. David Macey (New York: Picador, 2003), 27.

32. Stephen Pattison, *The Challenge of Practical Theology: Selected Essays* (London: Jessica Kingsley, 2007), 16.

33. Kwame Anthony Appiah, *The Ethics of Identity* (Princeton, NJ: Princeton University Press, 2005). Specifically chapter 5 titled, "Soul Making."

34. Kang, *Cosmopolitan Theology*, 7.

35. Rob Cover, *Queer Youth Suicide, Culture and Identity: Unliveable Lives?* (Burlington, VT: Ashgate, 2012), 139.

36. Kathleen Erwin, "Interpreting the Evidence: Competing Paradigms and the Emergence of Lesbian and Gay Suicide as a 'Social Fact,'" *International Journal of Health Services* 23, no. 3 (1993): 444.

37. Cover, *Queer Youth Suicide*, 139.

38. This is a central argument put forth in Thomas Joiner, *Why People Die By Suicide* (Cambridge: Harvard University Press, 2005).

39. Kelly Oliver, *Colonization of Psychic Space: A Psychoanalytic Social Theory of Oppression* (Minneapolis: University of Minnesota, 2004), 35.

40. Ian Burkitt, *Social Selves: Theories of Self and Society*, 2nd ed. (Los Angeles: SAGE, 2008), 54–55. Emphasis in original.

41. 5Burkitt, *Social Selves*, 54–5. Emphasis in original.

42. Findlay, *Caring for the Soul in a Postmodern Age*, 108–9.

43. Findlay, *Caring for the Soul in a Postmodern Age*, 40.

44. Muller criticizes social support models like the "It Gets Better" campaign, noting that it does not acknowledge the problems—such as heterosexism and transphobia and the attendant experiences of discrimination and violence—that LGBTQ youth face in their communities and focuses upon "idyllic outcomes" open only to those with the financial resources and social support necessary to make "sweeping changes in their environment after reaching adulthood." Amber Muller, "Virtual Communities and Translation into Physical Reality in the 'It Gets Better' Project," *Journal of Media Practice* 12, no. 3 (2011): 275.

45. Sharon D. Welch, *Communities of Resistance and Solidarity: A Feminist Theology of Liberation* (Maryknoll, NY: Orbis Books, 1985), 83.

46. Frank, "Practicing Dialogical Narrative Analysis," 50.

47. Kaufman, *An Essay on Theological Method*, ix.

48. Kaufman, *In Face of Mystery*, 434.

49. Welch, *Communities of Resistance and Solidarity*, 47.

50. Kang, *Cosmopolitan Theology*, 7.

51. Kang, *Cosmopolitan Theology*, 7.

52. Kang, *Cosmopolitan Theology*, 7.

53. Welch, *Communities of Resistance and Solidarity*, 7.

54. Welch, *Communities of Resistance and Solidarity*, 83.

55. Frank, "Practicing Dialogical Narrative Analysis," 50.

56. Kang, *Cosmopolitan Theology*, 7.

57. Cover, *Queer Youth Suicide*, 139.

58. Michael S. Hogue, "After the Secular: Toward a Pragmatic Public Theology," *Journal of the American Academy of Religion* 78(2) (June 2010), 348

59. Hogue, "After the Secular," 355.

60. Kang, *Cosmopolitan Theology*, 7.

Bibliography

Alison, James. *Broken Hearts & New Creations: Intimations of a Great Reversal.* New York: Continuum, 2010.

Alison, James. *Faith Beyond Resentment: Fragments Catholic and Gay.* New York: Crossroad, 2001.

Althaus-Reid, Marcella. "Queer I Stand: Lifting the Skirts of God." In *The Sexual Theologian: Essays on Sex, God and Politics.* Edited by Marcella Althaus-Reid and Lisa Isherwood, 99–109. New York: T&T Clark International, 2004.

Anderson, Herbert. "The Recovery of Soul." In *The Treasure of Earthen Vessels: Explorations in Theological Anthropology.* Edited by Brian H. Childs and David W. Waanders, 208–23. Louisville: Westminster John Knox Press, 1994.

Appiah, Kwame Anthony. *The Ethics of Identity.* Princeton, NJ: Princeton University Press, 2005.

Ashbrook, James B. *Minding the Soul: Pastoral Counseling as Remembering.* Minneapolis: Fortress, 1996.

Ashbrook, James B. "Soul: Its Meaning and Its Making." *Journal of Pastoral Care* 45, no. 2 (1991): 159–68.

Barnes David M. and Ilan H Meyer. "Religious Affiliation, Internalized Homophobia, and Mental Health in Lesbians, Gay Men, and Bisexuals." *American Journal of Orthopsychiatry* 82, no. 4 (2012): 505–15.

Bayard, Pierre. *How to Talk About Books You Haven't Read.* Translated by Jeffrey Mehlman. New York: Bloomsbury, 2007.

Bettelheim, Bruno. *Freud and Man's Soul.* New York: Vintage, 1982.

Bloch, Ernst. *Atheism in Christianity.* Translated by J. T. Swann. New York: Verso, 1972.

Brison, Susan J. *Aftermath: Violence and the Remaking of a Self.* Princeton, NJ: Princeton University Press, 2002.

Brown, Warren S. "Cognitive Contributions to Soul." In *Whatever Happened to the Soul? Scientific and Theological Portraits of Human Nature,* edited by Warren S. Brown, Nancey Murphy, and H. Newton Malony, 99–126. Minneapolis: Fortress Press, 1998.

Bruner, Jerome. *Acts of Meaning.* Cambridge, MA: Harvard University Press, 1990.

Burkitt, Ian. *Bodies of Thought: Embodiment, Identity & Modernity.* Thousand Oaks, CA: SAGE, 1999.

Burkitt, Ian. *Social Selves: Theories of Self and Society,* 2nd ed. Los Angeles: SAGE, 2008.

Butler, Judith. *Excitable Speech: A Politics of the Performative.* New York: Routledge, 1997.

Butler, Judith. *Precarious Life: The Powers of Mourning and Violence.* New York: Verso, 2004.

Butler, Judith. *Undoing Gender.* New York: Routledge, 2004.

Capps, Donald. "The Soul as the 'Coreness' of the Self." In *The Treasure of Earthen Vessels: Explorations in Theological Anthropology,* edited by Brian H. Childs and David W. Waanders, 82–104. Louisville: Westminster John Knox Press, 1994.

Cobb, Sara. *Speaking of Violence: The Politics and Poetics of Narrative in Conflict Resolution.* New York: Oxford, 2013.

Cooper-Lewter, Nicholas and Henry H. Mitchell. *Soul Theology: The Heart of American Black Culture.* Nashville, TN: Abingdon, 1991.

Copeland, M. Shawn. *Enfleshing Freedom: Body, Race, and Being.* Minneapolis: Fortress, 2010.

Cover, Rob. *Queer Youth Suicide, Culture and Identity: Unliveable Lives?* Burlington, VT: Ashgate, 2012.

Davaney, Sheila Greeve. *Pragmatic Historicism: A Theology for the Twenty-First Century.* Albany, NY: State University of New York Press, 2000.

Dorais, Michel. *Dead Boys Can't Dance: Sexual Orientation, Masculinity, and Suicide.* With Simon L. Lajeunesse. Translated by Pierre Tremblay. Montreal & Kingston: McGill-Queen's University Press, 2004.

Du Bois, W. E. B. *The Souls of Black Folk.* New York: Penguin Books, 1903/2018.

Eribon, Didier. *Insult and the Making of the Gay Self.* Translated by Michael Lucey. Durham, NC: Duke University Press, 2004.

Erwin, Kathleen. "Interpreting the Evidence: Competing Paradigms and the Emergence of Lesbian and Gay Suicide as a 'Social Fact.'" *International Journal of Health Services* 23, no. 3 (1993): 437–53.

Findlay, Edward F. *Caring for the Soul in a Postmodern Age: Politics and Phenomenology in the Though of Jan Patočka.* Albany, NY: State University of New York Press, 2002.

Flyvbjerg, Bent "Five Misunderstandings about Case-Study Research." In *Qualitative Research Practice.* Edited by Clive Seale, Giampetro Gobo, Jaber F. Gubrium, and David Silverman, 390–404. London: Sage, 2007.

Foucault, Michel. "The Ethics of the Concern of the Self as a Practice of Freedom." In *Ethics: Subjectivity and Truth.* Edited by Paul Rabinow. Translated by Robert Hurley, et al., 281–302. New York: The New Press, 1997.

Foucault, Michel. *Discipline & Punish: The Birth of the Prison.* Translated by Alan Sheridan. New York: Vintage Books, 1977.

Foucault, Michel. "Sex, Power, and the Politics of Identity." In *Ethics: Subjectivity and Truth.* Edited by Paul Rabinow. Translated by Robert Hurley, et al., 163–74. New York: The New Press, 1997.

Foucault, Michel. *Society Must Be Defended.* Translated by David Macey. New York: Picador, 2003.

Frank, Arthur W. *Letting Stories Breath: A Socio-Narratology.* Chicago: University of Chicago, 2010.

Frank, Arthur W. "Practicing Dialogical Narrative Analysis." In *Varieties of Narrative Analysis.* Edited by James Holstein and Jaber F. Gubrium, 33–52. Thousand Oaks, CA: SAGE, 2012.

Frankl, Viktor E. *The Doctor and the Soul: From Psychotherapy to Logotherapy.* Translated by Richard Winston and Clara Winston. New York: Vintage, 1986.

Freeman, Mark. *Hindsight: The Promise and Peril of Looking Backward.* New York: Oxford University Press, 2010.

Gerkin, Charles V. *The Living Human Document: Re-Visioning Pastoral Counseling in a Hermeneutical Mode.* Nashville: Abingdon, 1984.

Gerkin, Charles V. *Widening the Horizons: Pastoral Responses to a Fragmented Society.* Philadelphia: Westminster, 1986.

Goetz, Stewart and Charles Taliaferro. *A Brief History of the Soul.* Malden, MA: Wiley-Blackwell, 2011.

Graham, Elaine. *Words Made Flesh: Writings in Pastoral and Practical Theology.* London: SCM Press, 2009.

Graham, Larry Kent. *Care of Persons, Care of Worlds: A Psychosystems Approach to Pastoral Care and Counseling.* Nashville: Abingdon, 1992.

Grant, Jaime M., Lisa A. Mottet, and Justin Tanis. *Injustice at Every Turn: A Report of the National Transgender Discrimination Survey.* Washington, D.C.: National Center for Transgender Equality and National Gay and Lesbian Task Force, 2011.

Gross, Larry. "Out of the Mainstream: Sexual Minorities and the Mass Media." In *Gay People, Sex, and the Media,* edited by Michelle A. Wolf and Alfred P. Kielwasser, 19–46. New York: Harrington Park Press, 1991.

Hogue, Michael S. "After the Secular: Toward a Pragmatic Public Theology." *Journal of the American Academy of Religion* 78(2) (June 2010): 346–74.

Holstein, James A. and Jaber F. Gubrium. *The Active Interview*. Thousand Oaks, CA: SAGE, 1995.

Joiner, Thomas. *Why People Die By Suicide*. Cambridge: Harvard University Press, 2005.

Jung, C. G. *Modern Man in Search of a Soul*. Translated by W. S. Dell and Cary F. Baynes. New York: Harcourt, 1933.

Kang, Namsoon. *Cosmopolitan Theology: Reconstituting Planetary Hospitality, Neighbor-Love, and Solidarity in an Uneven World*. St. Louis: Chalice, 2013.

Kaufman, Gordon D. *An Essay on Theological Method*, 3rd ed. Atlanta, GA: Scholars Press, 1995.

Kaufman, Gordon D. *In Face of Mystery: A Constructive Theology*. Cambridge: Harvard University Press, 1993.

Kaufman, Gordon D. *Jesus and Creativity*. Minneapolis: Fortress, 2006.

King, Michael, Joanna Semlyne, Sharon See Tai, Helen Killaspy, David Osborn, Dmitri Popelyuk, and Irwin Nazareth. "A Systematic Review of Mental Disorder, Suicide, and Deliberate Self Harm in Lesbian, Gay and Bisexual People." *BCM Psychiatry* 8, no. 70 (2008): 1–17.

Laing, R. D. *The Divided Self: An Existential Study in Sanity and Madness*. Harmondsworth, UK: Penguin, 1960.

Lytle, Megan C., John. R. Blosnich, Susan M. De Luca, and Chris Brownson. "Association of Religiosity with Sexual Minority Suicide Ideation and Attempt." *American Journal of Preventive Medicine* 54, no. 5 (2018): 644–51.

Martin, Raymond and John Barresi. *The Rise and Fall of Soul and Self: An Intellectual History of Personal Identity*. New York: Columbia University Press, 2006.

Mayberry, Maralee. "The Story of a Salt Lake City Gay-Straight Alliance: Identity Work and LGBT Youth." *Journal of Gay & Lesbian Issues in Education* 4, no. 1 (2006): 13–31.

Miller-McLemore, Bonnie J. "The Living Human Web: Pastoral Theology at the Turn of the Century." In *Through the Eyes of Women: Insights for Pastoral Care*. Edited by Jeanne Stevenson Moessner, 9–26. Minneapolis: Fortress Press, 1996.

Muller, Amber. "Virtual Communities and Translation into Physical Reality in the 'It Gets Better' Project." *Journal of Media Practice* 12, no. 3 (2011): 269–77.

Nelson, Hilde Lindemann. *Damaged Identities, Narrative Repair*. Ithaca, NY: Cornell University Press, 2001.

Oliver, Kelly *Colonization of Psychic Space: A Psychoanalytic Social Theory of Oppression*. Minneapolis: University of Minnesota, 2004.

Patočka, Jan. *Body, Community, Language, World*. Translated by Erazim Kohák. Chicago: Open Court, 1998.

Pattison, Stephen. *The Challenge of Practical Theology: Selected Essays*. London: Jessica Kingsley, 2007.

Parker, Ian. *Qualitative Psychology: Introducing Radical Research*. New York: Open University Press, 2005.

Rank, Otto. *Psychology and the Soul: A Study of the Origin, Conceptual Evolution, and Nature of the Soul*. Translated by Gregory C. Richter and E. James Lieberman. New York: Johns Hopkins, 1930/1998.

Taylor, Charles. *Human Agency and Language: Philosophical Papers 1*. New York: Cambridge University Press, 1985.

Tsing, Anna Lowenhaupt. *The Mushroom at the End of the World: On the Possibility of Life in Capitalist Ruins*. Princeton, NJ: Princeton University Press, 2015.

U.S. Department of Health and Human Services (HHS) Office of the Surgeon General and National Action Alliance for Suicide Prevention. *2012 National Strategy for Suicide Prevention: Goals and Objectives for Action*. Washington, D.C., 2012.

Wagner, Glenn J., James Serafini, Judith Rabkin, Robert Remien, and Janet Williams. "Integration of one's religion and homosexuality: A weapon against internalized homophobia?," *Journal of Homosexuality* 26 (1994): 91–110.

Welch, Sharon D. *Communities of Resistance and Solidarity: A Feminist Theology of Liberation*. Maryknoll, NY: Orbis Books, 1985.

White, Mel. *Stranger at the Gate: To Be Gay and Christian in America*. New York: Plume, 1995.

White, Michael and David Epston. *Narrative Means to Therapeutic Ends*. New York: Norton, 1990.

Wood, Andrew William and Abigail Holland Conley. "Loss of Religious or Spiritual Identity Among the LGBT Population." *Counseling and Values* 59 (2014): 95–111.

Index

About the Author

Cody J. Sanders, PhD, is American Baptist Chaplain to Harvard University and Advisor for LGBTQ+ Affairs in the Office of Religious, Spiritual, & Ethical Life at the Massachusetts Institute of Technology. He also serves as pastor to Old Cambridge Baptist Church in Cambridge, MA. He has published several books including, *A Brief Guide to Ministry with LGBTQIA Youth.*